ALEXANDRA
PALACE

A HIDDEN HISTORY

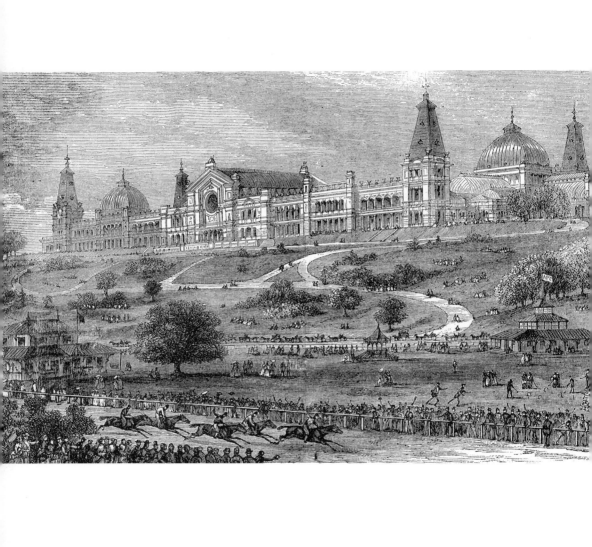

ALEXANDRA
PALACE
A HIDDEN HISTORY

Janet Harris

TEMPUS

Frontispiece *Alexandra Palace and racecourse, July 1875. The recently opened palace, replacing that burned down in 1873, promises a 'feast of delights in the sweet country air' which flows around the palace.*

First published 2005

Tempus Publishing Limited
The Mill, Brimscombe Port,
Stroud, Gloucestershire, GL5 2QG
www.tempus-publishing.com

British Library Cataloguing in Publication Data.
A catalogue record for this book is available from the British Library.

ISBN 0 7524 3636 8

Typesetting and origination by Tempus Publishing Limited.
Printed in Great Britain.

CONTENTS

Acknowledgements   6

Introduction   7

one   The Monster of Muswell Hill   9

two   Twentieth-Century Palace   25

three   In the Beginning   41

four   Ally Pally   47

five   Friends and Enemies   51

six   A German Civilian Prison   63

seven   Interned   71

eight   Inside the Wire   79

nine   Killing Time   95

ten   Hun Wives   103

eleven   Going Home   113

twelve   Aftermath   117

Epilogue   125

Index   126

ACKNOWLEDGEMENTS

This enterprise would never have come to fruition without the help and encouragement of the following good people.

Firstly, thanks to Deborah Hedgecock, Curator of Bruce Castle Museum who has been of the greatest assistance throughout. Combined with Katherine Burton of Tempus they have made a formidable team to keep me on track.

Archivist Libby Adams and Archive Assistant Jeff Gerhardt, both of Bruce Castle Archives, have cheerfully and tirelessly exhumed obscure documents for what seems like forever. My thanks also to Henry Jacobs, photographer, who did marvels in reproducing to a high standard some very unpromising material.

Many thanks to historian Ken Barker for his research on my behalf, veteran local historian Ken Gay of Hornsey Historical Society, Curator Ray Seal of the Metropolitan Police Museum, Mr Peyton Skipwith of the Fine Art Society and Peter and Jenny Towey, Vice-Presidents of the Anglo-German Family History Society who have provided advice on the most obscure topics of German history.

Organisations that have been mines of information and helpfulness include the British Library, the British Library Newspaper Library at Colindale, the Family Record Centre, the London Metropolitan Archives, the Imperial War Museum, the National Archives, the Library of the Religious Society of Friends and Alexandra Palace itself, where guided tours around the building help bring its history to life.

With grateful thanks to the following organisations who granted permission for the reproduction of illustrations: The Imperial War Museum for allowing reproduction of the Rudolf Sauter drawings on pages 87, 115 and 116, and the photograph of the unknown orchestra members on page 99; The Religious Society of Friends for the photographic reproduction of the members of the Alexandra Palace Arts and Handicrafts Committee on page 102; The London Metropolitan Archives for the reproductions on pages 83 and 88. The majority of the illustrations and documents have been provided by the genorosity of Haringey Museum and Archive Service at Bruce Castle, with the remainder being from the author's own collection.

Every possible effort has been made to trace all written sources within this volume. For veracity the original English and grammar, especially in the case of Richard Notschke, remains as written. The mis-spelling of Germans as 'Germhuns' by Horatio Bottomley in *John Bull* was deliberate.

The accuracy of the facts in this book has been checked as carefully as possible. However, original sources can contain errors, and memories fade over the years.

INTRODUCTION

Legend says that when the farmland upon which Alexandra Palace stands was sold, a curse was made that while nature would prosper on the site, man-made enterprises would fail. Over the past century and more, the history of the Palace has been chequered with troubles, with financial crises following hard upon each other.

Even for many who have never visited the Palace it is as well known to them as it is to those living nearby and attending regularly. Today the Palace is always busy, offering a huge variety of functions, from exhibitions to political rallies – indeed the very stuff the Palace was built to provide in the 1870s. The Palace is, as ever, a popular topic in local newspapers, with news items provoking letters that both praise and blame. Recent subjects for correspondence include reviving the racecourse and various suggestions to set the Palace on a new financial footing. The Palace Trustees appear at times to be as beleaguered as ever.

The echoes of history are everywhere. To help refurbish the theatre, a restoration project which has run out of capital, a concert to raise money for the enterprise with a performance of Handel's *Messiah* by professional musicians, singers and a choir was performed in the Great Hall in June 2005. In the same month the Palace was advertised to bidders who have viable proposals for running this historic building.

That is the future, now to the past. For the majority of people who use the Palace, or drive past, the building is part of the backdrop to their lives and famous for being the home of television, with the first broadcasts in 1936. Indeed, the studios are now a museum open to the public. Beyond this, knowledge of the Palace's history is sketchy. Yet this is a history rich in anecdote and human drama.

Publications on the Palace refer briefly, if at all, to the role played by it during the First World War. Few references are made to the fact that it was first home to Belgian refugees fleeing the invasion of their country in 1914. Any references to the period 1915 to 1919 records the Palace as being a military prisoner of war camp, and not its use as an internment camp for German and Austrian civilian men from 1915 to 1919.

My interest in the subject was sparked by the discovery that my great-uncle Carl Turk was one of these men. Imprisoned from 1915 to 1919, he was one of the many thousands who passed through its doors.

A plaque was erected in June 2000 to commemorate this period in the Palace's past. It is placed on the wall of what is known as the television tower. Provided by the Anglo-German Family History Society and unveiled by a lady whose father was one of the civilian internees, the ceremony was very moving. Pastor Volkmar Latosek, the German Lutheran pastor in London, made a brief speech.

The text of the plaque reads: '1914–1919. This plaque was placed here on Sunday 4 June 2000 by members of the Anglo-German Family History Society to remember over 17,000 German and other civilian prisoners of war interned at Alexandra Palace between 1914 and 1919, in particular those who died during that period'.

This volume tells their story.

Janet Harris
May 2005

❧ ONE ❧

THE MONSTER OF MUSWELL HILL

Tottenham Wood Farm stretched between the Middlesex villages of Mus Well, Wood Green and Hornsey. Named for the woods covering the Parish of Tottenham's heights, Roque's map of 1754 shows the woodlands occupying the site. William Robinson's *History of Tottenham* (1840) states that in 1789 the Lord of the Manor, the Earl of Coleraine, auctioned the land, described as: 'A freehold estate, consisting of Tottenham Wood, near Muswell Hill, the principal part of which was then cleared and cultivated'.

The purchaser, tobacconist Mr Mitchell of Norton Folgate, paid £11,400, building 'a good house' on the land and spending lavishly on improvements. Surviving until 1932, Mr Mitchell's farmhouse was used as the clubhouse for Muswell Hill golf club.

After Mr Mitchell's death, the property was owned by Thomas Rhodes, a great-uncle of African explorer Cecil Rhodes. Mr Rhodes developed the farm and in 1850 acquired an additional 450 acres following the construction of the new railway line from the adjacent Nightingale Hall estate, east of Tottenham Wood Farm.

After Thomas Rhodes' death at the age of ninety-three, the property went to his remaining family, which comprised his son's widow, her children, and Mr Rhodes' two daughters, one of whom was married. Thomas Rhodes outlived his son, also named Thomas, who died in 1846 aged forty-five. According to Thomas Rhodes Sr's will, after bequests, the residue of his estate was to be sold to pay debts and invested for the benefit of his grandchildren.

The Great Exhibition of 1851 in Hyde Park was a huge success and the exhibition building was subsequently moved from Hyde Park to Sydenham Hill in south-east London. A modified version of the building was re-erected, becoming known as the Crystal Palace and a centre for amusement. The success of the Great Exhibition bred many similar ventures, one of which was the International Exhibition at South Kensington in 1862, which soon failed.

With nothing in north London comparable to the Crystal Palace, in 1858 Owen Jones, the architect responsible for the interior decoration of the Crystal Palace, published a pamphlet displaying a glass structure he proposed to erect at Muswell Hill, as a north London Palace of the People. Owen Jones and others visited the site on 2 April 1859. The *Islington Gazette* of 23 June 1859 reported the site's inauguration by Lord Brougham on the 300ft hill on the Muswell Hill side on 16 June.

In March 1860 the Great Northern Palace Co. Ltd was formed and a ground plan published in the *Illustrated London News*. After an initial meeting nothing more was heard of the company.

Although still farmland, August 1860 saw the first public use of the estate. A Ragged Schools Festival, giving a holiday to the thousands of children who attended London's ragged schools, was held. The event failed. Catering was poor and disorganised and not even the musical efforts of the Victoria Rifles, Coldstream Guards and drum and fife bands of the East London and Whitechapel Shoeblack Brigade could save the day.

A prospectus from the North London Park & Land Co. Ltd, advertised in *The Times* of 16 August 1862, indicated a provisional contract for the Rhodes estate at £183,000 saying that: 'so far as the proposal goes, coupled with the well known eligibility of the site, there is nothing of a doubtful character in buying land at Wood Green at £400 an acre, and it would require extremely bad management to give the shareholders cause for regret hereafter'.

In 1863 the Alexandra Park Company was formed and acquired Tottenham Wood Farm to create a pleasure park and People's Palace, named for the Danish Princess Alexandra, who married the Prince of Wales (later King Edward VII) the same year.

The *North London News* of 25 July 1863 reported the opening of the Park with a Great Archery and Horticultural Fête on the lawn of Tottenham Wood House, with other festivities in the grounds of the recently acquired Muswell Hill's Grove Estate.

In 1865 the Alexandra Park Company went into liquidation, along with several others connected with the venture. Two new companies were formed – the Alexandra Palace Company and the Muswell Hill Company – both immediately beset by financial difficulties, including bankruptcies and unheeded funding appeals.

Emulating the Crystal Palace, parts of the 1862 South Kensington structure, including the gigantic dome, were purchased for re-erection at Muswell Hill. Following Alfred Meeson's design, construction of the new Palace began in September 1865, the Park being closed to the public in 1866 and 1867. Temporary brick kilns were erected, with field tramways running both to the building and neighbouring claypits. In the grounds a cricket pavilion, grandstand and a refreshment pavilion to hold 1,000 people were constructed, together with the racetrack and trotting ring

The first horse racing on the new track, immediately dubbed 'The Frying Pan' because of its shape, occurred on 30 June and 1 July, 1868. The meetings were unsuccessful. The high cost of attendance and the excessively hot weather – one day was 92°F in the shade and 122°F in the sun – plus the sun-baked hardness of the course, incurred much public criticism.

The Alexandra Palace Company published a prospectus naming 1 May 1869 for the opening of the Palace, as an auxiliary to the British Museum, the South

The Grove, c. 1860. The top-hatted gentleman is believed to be the owner, silk merchant William Block. Following his death in 1861, the Alexandra Park Company purchased the Grove in 1863, on which a people's palace was planned.

Kensington Museum and Kew Gardens. The public were invited to invest in 6 per cent preference shares to the value of £100,000. The public flatly refused the invitation. Unable to offload the shares, plans were scrapped for the 1869 opening, the Palace and Park remaining closed to the public for several years.

A tontine, launched on 22 July 1871, was advertised in *Punch*. Despite extensive publicity and free lectures on the benefits of public subscription to the tontine, *The Times* of 15 November announced the tontine's failure, assuring subscribers their investment would be fully repaid. Another attempt to attract the disinterested public had failed.

In November 1872, a request by the Lord Mayor of London to the wealthy for £100,000 to purchase the Palace and grounds met massive indifference.

Bedevilled by soil subsidence – one building foreman described 'the nearby hills slipping around like anything' – on one rainy night a hill moved downwards by 3ft, while another wet night saw the downward movement of nearly 4 acres. Finally the building was completed.

The first Palace. Destroyed by fire on 9 June 1873.

The Palace of the People opened to the public on Queen Victoria's fifty-fourth birthday, 24 May 1873. The inaugural ceremonies included a magnificent concert, featuring some of the leading singers of the time. Another attraction was the organ, built by Henry Willis. A report in the *Illustrated London News* of 31 May 1873 stated:

> The opening last Saturday of the Alexandra Palace and Park, was a pleasant festival to many thousands of Londoners... The grounds are situated in the most agreeable part of Middlesex, exactly six miles from Charing Cross, but amidst rural scenery of delightful freshness, variety and beauty... The new railway line from King's Cross to Alexandra Palace is most convenient, giving access to it by a station platform directly beneath the main entrance, with an ascent by a few steps to the central transept.

In the first two weeks the Palace had over 120,000 visitors, many using the new railway, the 1s return fare from King's Cross included admission to the Palace. The venture was deemed a great success and a brilliant future forecast.

Around midday on Monday 9 June, disaster struck. The People's Palace caught fire. Differing accounts attribute the blame to a variety of causes, all allegedly man-made, in particular workmen on the roof at the time. Excerpts from a report in the *Weekly Herald* of 14 June describe the events:

> A little cloud, no bigger than a man's hand seemed the indication of the approaching catastrophe in the dome. The faint reflection developed into a lurid glare ... two minutes would have sufficed to convince them [onlookers] of the extent and nature of the danger... As it was, the 500-odd persons who were in the Palace on Monday ... behaved in the

An artist's impression of the blaze.

most admirable manner, and amidst the lurid glare which began to overspread the roof, and the warning crackle of the gathering flames, the building was quietly evacuated without disorder or confusion. Grand was the spectacle of the flames, curling and wreathing themselves around the framework of the roof, and closing round the building in their terrible embrace, filling it with dense, rolling volumes of smoke, soiling and blackening the elaborate and costly embellishments, before the lambent tongues of flame actually encircled them.

The report continues with details of the retrieval of objects and then goes on:

In the meantime a rush was made to the hydrants … but unfortunately the Palace had to pay the penalty of its lofty and commanding position, and it was found impracticable to obtain a fresh supply of water, owing to the ground. The firemen, unable to project the water to a sufficient height, had to limit their efforts to flooding the floor, with a view to retard the work of destruction as much as possible. In less than half an hour after the first alarm had been given, the whole interior was one dense seething mass of fire, belching forth huge lambent tongues of flame, and surmounted by black, whirling columns of smoke, which even from afar towered high above the horizon and became a conspicuous object for miles around. The great organ and the orchestral amphitheatre were at the same time crushed beneath the great mass of falling debris. When the steam engines, which arrived under Captain Shaw, together with the village engines and two engines sent by special train from King's Cross were on the spot the Palace no longer existed. The whole available force of the Wood Green district, numbering twenty-four men, with Inspector Gray and Sergeants Tuppenny and Malone were on the spot within twenty minutes after the first alarm had been given.

Ruins after the fire.

The burned out shell.

Surprisingly, given the speed with which the fire spread, there were few deaths. Thomas Larner (49), foreman of the smiths, died on 12 June from his injuries. These occurred when Mr Larner and another smith, Thomas Page, were hurrying from the blaze when a large part of the burning building fell upon them. Despite being badly injured, Mr Page attempted to rescue Mr Larner and helped carry him to a pony cart which took him to hospital. John Kelsey (57), a plateman in the employment of the Palace's caterers, died due to smoke suffocation during the blaze.

The Palace night-watchman, believed to be Richard Jordan, was also reported missing while attempting to douse the fire with buckets of water when the building collapsed. It was assumed his remains would never be recovered, as he had been in the burning Palace.

Unsurprisingly, before the day was out, people were arrested for looting some of the rescued items. Debris from the fire, blown by the wind, scattered for miles, some landing in Essex, and still being recovered several days later. In Epping Forest schoolboys found programmes, menu cards and posters.

The Graphic of 14 June 1873 reported an eye witness saying: 'The dome was thoroughly alight when the fire engine was brought in and talk of penny squirts and farthing fountains, it stood no more chance of touching the flames than you would of throwing a jug of water over a parish church'.

A letter dated 10 June from Thomas Dixon, Secretary of the Alexandra Palace Company was published in the same *Weekly Herald* that reported the fire. This stated that at a meeting on 10 June, it was agreed the Palace would be rebuilt, and architect John Johnson, who had worked with Meeson on the first Palace, would prepare new designs and planned outside events would continue during the rebuilding.

The editorial in the *Weekly Herald* of 21 June reported that the Alexandra Palace Company had issued a prospectus inviting the public to subscribe £150,000 in 6 per cent first preference shares in order to build a new Palace. The report concludes: 'We feel sure that no argument of ours is needed to induce our readers to respond to the invitation contained in the prospectus referred to'. Readers refused the invitation: the issue flopped.

Work on clearing the site began in July, with about 200 workmen engaged in the demolition. Two labourers removing portions of collapsed wall made a gruesome discovery. They found women's clothing and a mass of rags, bones and flesh in a very advanced state of decomposition. Tangled in the remains were jewellery, two umbrellas and ladies' purses.

The *Tottenham and Edmonton Advertiser* of 1 September covered the inquest of 23 August at the Alexandra Park Tavern. PC John Bolding who had been on duty at the Palace on 25 June stated that he had been patrolling the 6ft-high barriers erected around the ruins to prevent illegal entry. Hearing a tremendous crash and, not realising anyone was nearby, he assumed the weakened structure caused the collapse. Other witnesses verified his account. The paper described the inquest:

The remains were lying in an outhouse adjoining the tavern, and the fact was sufficiently indicated by the effluvium, which from time to time diffused itself about, much to the discomfiture of the jurymen, who went through the formality of viewing the bodies, which

Above: *Found in the wreckage – a presentation tankard dated June 1873.*

Left: *The first theatre – damaged by the fire.*

were completely covered with powerful disinfectants. Of the bodies themselves, nothing remained but a confused mass of remnants of clothing and decayed flesh and bones, the whole of a dull, dark uniform colour, produced by the solution of mingled moisture and brick dust, to the action of which the bodies had been exposed. This ghastly duty being performed, the jury returned to the inconveniently small room in the tavern set apart for such purposes and crowded to suffocation.

The inquest jury concluded that the women, sisters Mrs Sarah Everett (47) and Mrs Maria Constable (55) had died from suffocation caused by the accidental falling of a wall on them. The coroner recorded a verdict of 'accidental death'.

Using the same site, and some of the original materials, John Johnson redesigned and constructed a larger building of seven acres at a final cost of £417,128. By January 1874 about 800 men were in constant employment and half a dozen steam engines operational. A provisional re-opening date of 22 June 1874 was set.

A tragic death occurred in April 1874. Men were engaged on moulding and ornamental work when suddenly, without warning, about 70ft of the stucco work collapsed, taking with it men, scaffolding and bricks and some of the thick iron water pipes that were being installed. A bricklayer named Abraham Branch lost his life. At the inquest on 21 April the wife swore the body was her husband's but upon being pressed stated she had not been permitted to view it to identify it. The doctor said she had seen it and acknowledged it, whereupon the coroner took some offence and left the room in a huff saying he knew how to conduct his business, the inquest being postponed. When the inquest was resumed a verdict of 'accidental death' was recorded. The deceased was not only a bricklayer but was also the landlord of the West Green beerhouse at West Green Tottenham and a highly respected member of the Ancient Order of Foresters. With the band of the 33rd Middlesex Rifle Volunteers heading the procession he was buried on Sunday 1 May. This new style of musical burial caused outrage to some Sabbatarians and unruly scenes allegedly occurred.

Another fatality happened on 16 June when bricklayer James Kennedy struck his head against a plank, missed his footing and fell to the ground.

At a meeting of the Palace directors on 5 June 1874 the original deadline for opening was deemed impossible, so postponement until early 1875 was agreed.

After the inadequate water supply to the first building, the new design incorporated four water tanks placed on the four corner towers, each holding more than 16,000 gallons. The angles of the central hall contained four reservoirs of 7,000 gallons each, the whole being supplied by steam pumps from the New River Company's nearby reservoirs. Other fire prevention measures were incorporated in the new design. A novelty was the introduction of flush lavatories; thirty-four ladies' and forty-six gentlemen's divided between the four corners of the building.

The grand central hall, 386ft long by 184ft wide, with a central vaulted roof span of 85ft could accommodate an audience of 12,000 and an orchestra of 2,000. A series of brightly coloured statues of England's rulers, from William the Conqueror to Queen Victoria, including Oliver Cromwell, ranged along the sides of the central hall, all wearing the 'regal costume of their period' and illustrating a remarkable event in their lives. The side walls bore armorial bearings of principal cities and towns. The focal point of the hall was the rebuilt Willis organ which was allegedly the principal organ in size, design and equipment. Driven by two steam engines, of 8 and 12hp, with vast bellows housed in the basement, twenty-four hours' notice was required for the raising of steam before the organ could be used, either for playing or tuning. The hall's acoustics were deemed by 'eminent authorities' to be perfect.

A further attraction was the installation, adjacent to the central hall, of the Palace's very own post and telegraph office from which one could be 'in direct telegraphic communication with the Metropolis and all parts of the Kingdom as well as with foreign countries'. The Palace also boasted a fire station partly manned by staff volunteers; a police office and lost property office. The London Stereoscopic Company 'had been entrusted with the sole right of photography, and suitable studios provided for the purpose'.

Under the management of Sir Edward Lee, the second Palace opened on 1 May 1875. Trains were restored, including a service from Broad Street. On the first day 21,000 visitors were recorded. The following Whit Monday notes 94,000 visitors, many of whom travelled to the Palace by rail. The journey from King's Cross took over an hour and on the evening return journey a derailment caused some to walk off the railway while others slept on the trains.

The programme promised an astonishing variety of events – both inside and outside – until December. External attractions included cricket, an outdoor swimming pool and the Denayrouze Diving Pavilion near the Palace's east entrance, comprising a tank containing nearly forty tons of water wherein several divers would entertain visitors 'with the various and latest in the art of diving'. The Pavilion was described as a building similar to that constructed for the Paris Exhibition of 1867.

The Grove.

The refreshment departments were under the supervision of Messrs Bertram and Roberts, who promised that 'this important department will be conducted in a style which will surpass any other English or foreign establishments of the kind'. Besides the grand dining hall designed to seat 1,000, in the Park stood a banqueting hall with provision for 1,500 diners. There were many other dining and refreshment facilities scattered throughout the grounds, while separate arrangements had been made for the servants of visitors to the Palace.

Boating on the lakes, walks in the Grove, accompanied by al fresco musical performances on the bandstand, visits to the Japanese village, the modern Moorish house and modern Egyptian house helped while away the hours.

Horses, fruit and flowers, dogs, pigeons, poultry and cage birds were among promised shows. Archery competitions, cycle races, fireworks, swings and a skating rink were a few of the attractions advertised, plus a circus ring capable of seating 3,000 for equestrian performances. Alongside accommodation for the circus animals was stabling for 400 visitors' horses. Indoors, a theatre seating more than 3,000 was allegedly as large as Drury Lane. For the highbrow there were concerts, operas, oratorios, choirs, a resident orchestra, recitals on the Willis organ and exhibitions of paintings and other works of art.

Despite the variety of entertainment the gigantic enterprise was a financial disaster. Dependent upon a steady flow of visitors, it was only Sundays and bank holidays that attracted large numbers, otherwise there were low levels of public attendance, especially during the winter months. The Palace's concept – to cater for the education and leisure of the masses – overlooked the fact that the masses wanted entertainment rather than education and had very little money or leisure, despite six bank holidays established by Act of Parliament in 1871.

A royal visit on 20 June 1876 gave a brief boost to attendances. On the first day of the horse show the Prince of Wales, the Duke of Connaught and the 'elite of the nobility' were in attendance. At 1.20 p.m. the drag of the Duke of Beaufort, carrying HRH The Prince of Wales, with Lord Arthur Somerset 'handling the ribbons' entered by the Muswell Hill Gate. Lord Carrington's drag conveyed HRH The Duke of Connaught.

With debts from the underwriting of the first Palace, no income during rebuilding, high maintenance and heating charges and, even if there were few visitors, employees' wages to be met, the Alexandra Palace Company was wound up in October 1876 and sold in 1877 to the London Financial Association (LFA). Offered for sale with a reserve price of £600,000 the highest bid received was £450,000. In May 1877, while never running the Palace themselves, LFA posed as proprietors and with Bartram and Roberts as lessees, the Palace re-opened for visitors. This would be the first of many ventures, most of which failed. The LFA's policy was to lease the enterprise to anyone willing to take the risks involved. In July 1877 the Alexandra Palace Act was quietly slipped through Parliament by 'friends' and seemingly ignored by the newspapers. This Act allowed the LFA to sell a portion of the Palace land if necessary. Using these powers the LFA sold 80 acres on the north of the Palace for house building. In 1878 and the 1880s a few plots for villas were sold and roads laid out, but it would be several years before Muswell Hill started developing.

In early 1880 Bartram and Roberts gave notice of terminating their tenancy in May. The Palace re-opened in May under James Willing, closing in October. In December 1880 entertainments manager William Henry Jones and Benjamin Barber, the Park's refreshments contractor, acquired the lease of the foundering enterprise. On Boxing Day they mounted 'a big programme for twelve hours enjoyment for twelve pence'. Attractions included Princess Newuramoosha of the Osage and other North American Indians showing Indian ways, plus a female walking contest between Mesdames Victor, Engles and Florence. For the next two seasons, Jones and Barber brought record attendances to Palace and Park, mostly of the middle and working classes, the anticipated high class carriage trade rarely materialising.

Barber, altering the refreshment tariff, introduced buffets, bars and second- and third-class refreshment rooms, knowing that working-class visitors wanted fast food – but the food was never fast enough. There were hellish rows with hungry cockneys who wanted only a hard boiled egg and a cup of tea.

Jones attempted to lure visitors on the normally slack weekdays and lengthy off-seasons. He retained a permanent circus company, panoramas and nightly firework displays, plus a bill of artistes who could be detached for performances anywhere within the Palace and grounds. But many of Jones's weekday performers belonged to the realm of 'self-improving rational diversions' featuring cooking lessons by Mrs Gothard, clay-pipe making, sheep-

A visit to the second Palace by the Prince of Wales on 20 June 1876.

dog trials, exhibitions of goat and rabbit breeding (not to each other), and demonstrations of the very latest industrial machinery, including hourly exhibitions of the Palace's own food refrigerators and ice-making equipment. Visitors never materialised.

On their first August bank holiday in 1880, nearly 108,000 paid admission to the Palace and Park. This would be the largest number the Palace would ever see on a single day.

The next year got off to a good start. Good Friday attracted 25,000 for concerts of sacred music conducted by Meyer Lutz. On Easter Monday, paid admission was 76,000. For the Whit Monday bank holiday on 6 June, Jones and Barber devised a yard-long playbill ruled in inches so that 'it would be retained in households as a useful item' and announcing that the bill was one of '100,000 printed, one for each expected visitor'. The bill promised plenty of free seats, comfort, amusements and refreshments for 100,000 visitors and listed a timetable of events, train schedules and excursion ticket prices, restaurant tariffs and that there were amusements inside, outside, over and under the Palace for 100,000 visitors!

Offered as wholly free spectacles were 'The Destruction of the Spanish Armada' contrived by fireworks manufacturer James Paine using model ships, live actors with rockets and red fire on the great lake. Two matches of clown cricketers could be viewed from the racecourse grandstand, while swimmers Professor and Mrs Parker and their one-legged pupil would amaze. Other activities included professional boxing and wrestling tournaments, Scuri on his unicycle, aerialists Lolo, Sylvester and Lola would defy gravity in the Great Hall, while balloonist Captain Morton would attempt the same outdoors, ascending heavenwards from the grounds.

The rebuilt Willis organ in the Great Hall of the second Palace.

The circus amphitheatre was utilised for Boucicault's melodrama *The Streets of London*, the scene of the tenement fire and Badger's timely rescue of the incriminating document given veracity by the skills of the Wood Green fire brigade and their horse-drawn pumper.

Musical tastes were catered for by band and ballad concerts, while the theatre was a turmoil of activity.

Dr Holden would perform his conjuring tricks hourly, while 'Little Salvini, the wonderful child actor' offered a repeating programme of popular recitations. In the Lecture Room, Adonis, the Lilliputian African Prince, promised hourly receptions.

On the hot and overcast day, by late afternoon over 90,000 visitors had paid to enter the Palace. Crowds, camping outside the Park gates began passing through the turnstiles from 9.00 a.m. By the afternoon the weather had changed and at 6.00 p.m. those gathering to watch Captain Morton's ascent were caught in the first shower, which soon turned to heavy, persistent rain. Soaking visitors crowded indoors, jamming theatres, galleries and refreshment rooms but were soon fighting for places on the London-bound trains. Although the day finished in typical English fashion, Jones and Barber's programme had attracted a tide of paying visitors.

A newspaper advertisement offered meetings of the Alexandra Park Foxhounds on Tuesday 15 and Saturday 19 November 1881. The *Weekly Herald* of 9 December reported that events of 15 November saw Jones and Barber defending themselves to the Edmonton Bench on 5 December. The RSPCA, under the Cruelty to Animals Act, summoned the two men, alleging the 'sport' advertised at the Palace was cruelty and that many complaints were received by the Society to this effect. On 15 November an RSPCA inspector had visited the 'hunt' and observing that instead of the advertised fox (which, it seems, was the usual quarry) a stag, kept specifically for the purpose, was released into the Palace grounds and pursued by three gentlemen, a lady and a pack of dogs. After a short chase the dogs seized the stag and 'tore and mauled at it' until driven off. Upon examination by the Society's officer, the stag was found to be bleeding freely and suffering from several wounds and then chained to railings and left alone for 'some considerable time'. Jones and Barber conceded this hunt had been an experiment, they had not realised they would be inflicting animal cruelty as usually they 'allowed the animal to get out of the grounds as the hunt often extended over ten or twelve miles.' In a letter to the court, Jones and Barber promised that all future hunts would involve drag hunting only.

The bench concluded there was no necessity for further proceedings after the publicity given to the matter, and the explanation of Jones and Barber.

The 1882 season started with bad weather. Admission was raised from 1s to 2s 6d. Attractions included free admission to the circus ring, to see the Perks family and other good riders, clowns and 'a marvellous performance with Myer's celebrated lions and elephants, including Blind Bill, the largest elephant in Europe'. In November with £11,200 of rent arrears, the partners filed for liquidation. Jones died in March 1883.

In July 1883 the Palace and grounds were put up for auction. There were no takers. The Palace remained closed through 1884, with the Park open to the public. On 31 May 1885 the Palace opened as an International Exhibition Centre and closed three months later on 5 September. The Palace remained closed in 1886. The *North Middlesex Chronicle* of 17 April describes Easter when the grounds were opened to the public:

FIFTH OF NOVEMBER AT THE ALEXANDRA PALACE

Fox hunting was one of the attractions advertised for 5 November 1881.

But the grass grown paths, the fast closed vacant building, the unkempt grounds and railway station almost decaying for want of paint, seemed to spread a melancholy atmosphere even over the merry groups who were trying to amuse themselves with skipping ropes, swings and a solitary steam roundabout that refused to perform its circumlocutory duties.

Not even the grounds were open for the August bank holiday.

A new venture began on East Monday 1887 with lessee Mr W.H. Hayward, closing before the year end after a disastrous season.

Milkmen were encouraged to distribute free admission tickets with their daily deliveries. With the Palace's bad reputation for mismanagement and poor catering the public refused them. Nothing would induce people who had once visited the Palace, either season ticket holders or those offered free admission, to return a second time. A standing joke of the day went 'that in lieu of six months hard [labour] an extra severe magistrate gave sentences of a Palace season ticket'.

The years 1888–89 saw openings and rapid closures of both Park and Palace. The *Licensed Victuallers' Gazette* of 21 September 1888 wrote that Alexandra Palace had 'struck it at last' in respect of American balloonist Professor Baldwin's benefit of 13 September, which 100,000 people attended. *Emtrach*, writing on 29 September stated:

Professor Baldwin no doubt attracted a large number of spectators to the Alexandra Palace, but the ordinary type of show is of no use whatsoever there. As I have said a score of times, it is only an extraordinary bait that will entice people to Muswell Hill, and extraordinary baits are not always to be had. In the absence of Mr Baldwin it will be found that the Alexandra Palace is considerably deserted.

The Palace's proprietors constantly complained of crowds gathering outside the grounds for these ascents and firework displays rather than coming in and spend money.

In October 1888, viewed by the Prince and Princess of Wales, together with Princesses Louise, Victoria and Maude, Professor Baldwin parachuted from a balloon at 5,000ft.

Except for occasional events in the grounds, the years of 1890 to 1897 saw the Palace and Park closed. Queen Victoria's Diamond Jubilee in June 1897 was not celebrated beyond horse racing. The only acknowledgement of the Jubilee was the attending band striking up the National Anthem.

An article in *London* of 7 October 1897 portrayed the grounds as neglected, weed-strewn and heavily wooded, occupied by only a herd of cattle. The Great Hall is described as:

still resplendent with its gold and many coloured frescos, circular window of coloured glass, palms, statues, all seeming as though the last entertainment had taken place yesterday instead of eight years ago. The Great Hall's only occupants are the highly coloured and labelled monarchs of England, standing on each side of the transept.

On Good Friday 1898 the Palace re-opened, closing on 5 November. A brief season ran from 31 March to 30 September 1899. To celebrate the new century the Palace and Park opened occasionally, permanently closing in October 1900.

❧ TWO ❧

TWENTIETH-CENTURY PALACE

Proposals to sell the Park for homes caused such public outrage that legislation giving the Park and Palace into public ownership was passed under the Alexandra Park and Palace (Public Purposes) Act of 1900.

A board of Trustees, representing various local authorities, was led by Henry Burt JP, of Middlesex County Council. The board immediately discovered that a lease with option of purchase was being granted to a speculative syndicate, and that if the property was to be secured for public use, rapid action was required. Only twenty-four hours were granted for the raising of a deposit of £5,000 payment and an agreement, giving option for purchase, was signed. Two Trustees and other local dignitaries provided the deposit. A sum totalling £150,000 was required and raised by local county and district councils.

The *Morning Leader* of 13 April 1901 announced the re-opening of the Palace: 'Free to all for the first time on 13 May. In fact, the hope is to make the Palace a free resort without parallel, a home of happiness, health and culture. There are to be free picture galleries, museums, music, organ recitals, choir festivals, bands, entertainments and exhibitions of all kinds of the earth's wonders and marvels man has produced'.

The grand opening began with a musical selection from the Alexandra Palace Military Band, followed by a fanfare from the Royal State Trumpeters heralding the arrival of His Grace the Duke of Bedford in the Great Hall, from where he declared the Palace and Park open. At dusk the Alexandra Palace Military Band assembled on the South Terrace for the firework display, advertised by Brock's as 'Novel designs for the new century', beginning with a Signal Aerial Maroon 'exploding at a great height and announcing the commencement of the display'.

Entertainments included picture illusionists Professor Thomas and Madame Louie Howard – 'Marvellous exponents of the art of thought reading and second sight'. (In view of later events it is unfortunate the Trustees did not offer them immediate permanent employment).

The Avenue, before being sold for house building. The circus ring is to the left but out of the picture.

Maude Evan's Silver Moon Pierrots were in the Bijou Theatre, with a 'swimming tank performance' and an 'assault at arms' offered, plus a variety of refreshments being provided by the Bertram Brothers. The final page of the programme advertised attractions until Boxing Day. As the Trustees had spent all the capital on purchasing and refurbishing the building and grounds no reserves existed for upkeep and maintenance, so they were financially dependent on visitors.

By July the Palace was in debt. A loan of £3,000 plus an overdraft secured for an unlimited amount were obtained. The continuous, free weekday entertainments generated huge financial losses and, by the end of the first year, the enterprise was even further in debt. There was much public anger towards the Trustees.

Islington Trustee Charles Townley, better known in theatrical circles as Geoffrey Thorne and the only Committee member with practical experience of public entertainment, was highly critical of Henry Burt's plan to have continuous entertainment until the year's end. The *Topical Times* of 27 July 1901 reported him as saying: 'I ask any man of common sense how many people are likely to go to the Palace after the close of summer? The Palace is essentially a summer resort, and in my opinion it is absolute folly to spend money on winter catering'.

Taking up Townley's theme, the same edition of the *Topical Times* criticised the entertainment, referring to 'a mediocre band playing continuously to a beggarly array of empty benches. The management has made the Palace a dumping ground for second rate amusements … what, for instance, can be more disconcerting than in strolling in the Italian Garden to be suddenly confronted by a group of busking Sambos and their bones and burnt cork, who are ill suited to a paradise of palms and fernery? Nor, from an aesthetic point of view, is the statuary improved by being turned into bill-posting stations'.

The skating rink – a popular attraction.

The opening of the roller–skating rink failed to halt the decline. *The Star* of 21 September 1901 announced: 'Winter Joys at the Alexandra Palace' and a 'magnificent skating rink has been laid down in the conservatory, with a polished maple floor of 130ft by 92ft. The skates to be used are of the new pneumatic ball-bearing type. To be opened to the public from 5 October'.

King Edward VII's Coronation in 1902 provided a boost to the Palace and Park. The *Morning Leader* of 24 April 1902 reported that the War Office had accepted the Alexandra Palace Trustees' offer to accommodate the Colonial troops for the Coronation Festival, and 'in a few weeks' time the grounds will be studded with tents and picturesque with the brilliant and distinctive uniforms of many nationalities'. The newspaper described the catering and sleeping accommodation being provided for the 2,500 troops, of whom 750 were men of colour. Readers were informed that troops who required special diets and insisted on cooking it themselves, would receive the raw materials to cook at their own camp fires. A consequence of this was a widespread shortage of chickens for the Indian troops, who preferred to kill and prepare the birds themselves. The *Wood Green Sentinel* of 26 September reported that suppliers had to go ever farther afield. Arrangements had been made for the tethering of 2,000 horses in a field adjoining the Grove.

The Coronation was delayed until August to allow the King's recovery from surgery. Consequently, the troops were in residence from May to September. Financial worries were constant for the Trustees. The *Wood Green Sentinel* of 3 October 1902 reported staffing costs of £300 per week. The *Hornsey and Finsbury Park Journal* of 11 October reported on the Palace from 1 March 1901 to 30 April 1902:

The winter was a season of heavy loss – can the public be attracted to the Palace during the months of bad weather? In midwinter the walk through the Park is somewhat dreary, even in

Choral performance in the Great Hall.

the early hours, while late at night it is far from pleasant to turn out into the darkness to make the journey home. The Park is little better than a wilderness. The Trustees have succeeded in putting the building into a creditable state of repair. They have warmed it, lighted it, have shut off the draughts that were only too demonstrative during the early part of last winter and nobody need go to the Palace without finding something to interest and amuse.

The *Islington Gazette* of 8 October said of the Colonial troops' occupation: 'The Park is now a waste, destroyed by the camps of the Colonial troops, with roads and paths now made quagmires and the shrubbery destroyed'. Newspapers complained that: 'Even on a fine day, [one cannot walk here] without showing traces similar to those left by a stroll across a ploughed field. On a wet day, well, the less said about that the better'.

November 1902 saw the opening of a velodrome in the Central Transept, the only indoor cycling track outside America, the nearest being at Madison Square Gardens in New York. Despite bad weather, more than three thousand attended the first night. The velodrome failed, closing in February.

The Trustees were heavily dependent upon catering income. Bertram's catering promises in the 1901 opening programme – which noted that 'much remains to be done before it [the catering] can be considered satisfactory' – were so regularly broken that few thought the matter worthy of comment.

Above, right: *Colonial troops in the grounds of Alexandra Palace.*

Centre, right: *Colonial troops out walking.*

Below, right: *Colonial troops in the Banqueting Hall.*

Below: *Colonial troops in the grounds of Alexandra Palace.*

An article entitled 'How the Palace Caters: A Biter Bit' appeared in the *North Middlesex Chronicle* of 9 May 1903 brought this sorry state of affairs to public notice:

It was noon on May Day and I wended my way into the second class refreshment room ... [the room] was spacious and lofty, but very dreary and inhabited by large tables covered with dirty cloths. The whole appearance was so uninviting that had it not been for the bright manner of the waitresses traversing some four miles of plank flooring to minister to the needs of about half a dozen May Dayers spread about the room, I fear I would have fled. Replying to my request for two boiled eggs the waitress said 'certainly' and flitted out of the room. Some twenty minutes later the waitress returned flushed and breathless, carrying a tray which bore two eggs, one reposed in a long-stemmed wine glass instead of an egg cup. Upon recovering, she said: 'I hope you'll excuse me, sir, but I could not find an egg cup and had to bring the egg in this'. I assured her the egg would be just as good eaten from a wine glass as an egg cup. After foraging around, she procured a plate and knife. I dug my spoon in the egg in the wine glass. When its odour began to crawl down the side of the glass and mount high into the atmosphere, I felt it would have been better served in a factory chimney. I removed the first egg and raised the other in its stead. There are evidently degrees of badness in eggs as there are in other things, and if that of the first was positive the second was comparative. The waitress came up and divining the problem asked if she should get anther egg. I did not care to risk it again but she insisted, and after a certain amount of time reappeared with the third. Its chief characteristic was that of the other two but superlative.

As I was sorrowfully finishing my tea, roll and butter, a man came across the room enquiring had I seen a salt cellar wandering that way. I informed him I had briefly possessed one but someone had borrowed it, and the last time I saw it, it was slowly making its way to a little boy at the other end of the room. He turned away with saddened gaze, and continued his weary search. Then another came, requesting mustard, without even a word of hope. And thus these saddened men came and went.

It was a remarkable thing that though the great Labour Festival was being held, hardly a dozen people came in for refreshments. I was reflecting on this and hardly had the speculation traversed the whole of my still egg-fume fighting brain when some thirty children and five adults entered, spreading themselves over the chairs. I trembled violently for fear they should ask for anything in the eating line stronger than buns, and the waitresses paled in anticipation. The suspense only lasted for a moment; they had evidently bitten there and been bitten the year before, for one of the men suddenly produced a capacious hamper and divided its contents among the crowd'.

This article prompted a huge response – none of which was favourable to the Palace catering. 'Tea' was described by one visitor as execrable while butter was stretched to sixty pats to the pound. Later, after attending a meeting, the visitor indulged in a small whiskey and soda, price 6d. He asked the barmaid whether she had omitted to add the whisky. Her reply was to the point: 'What d'yer expects goin' to piy for the plice?' He thought this was hard after paying 1s to enter the Palace, concluding: 'No more Alexandra Palace for me, scores of people go once and refuse to go again to be fleeced'.

Refreshments.

𝕿𝖍𝖊 𝕯𝖎𝖓𝖎𝖓𝖌 𝖆𝖓𝖉 𝕽𝖊𝖋𝖗𝖊𝖘𝖍𝖒𝖊𝖓𝖙 𝕽𝖔𝖔𝖒𝖘 are situated on the South side of the Buildings in both the East and West wings.

During the evening a 𝕿𝖆𝖇𝖑𝖊 𝖉'𝖍𝖔𝖙𝖊 𝕯𝖎𝖓𝖓𝖊𝖗 will be served in the East wing dining room.

𝕿𝖍𝖊 𝕲𝖗𝖎𝖑𝖑 𝕽𝖔𝖔𝖒 adjoining will be open for Teas, Grill and cold viands.

𝕷𝖎𝖌𝖍𝖙 𝕽𝖊𝖋𝖗𝖊𝖘𝖍𝖒𝖊𝖓𝖙𝖘 are served at the small tables outside the long refreshment counters at the East and West wings.

Messrs. W. & J. H. BERTRAM desire to say that they have been allowed only a very limited time, quite insufficient, to furnish and equip the Refreshment department, and that much remains to be done before it can be considered satisfactory, and they therefore ask the indulgence of the visitors especially on this first day and for a few days longer while the remaining rooms are being put in order.

Refreshments – extract from a catering advertisement from the 1901 opening programme.

In June, the auditors reported the first year of operation, showing a total loss of £2,735 reduced to £735 by Mr Burt's contribution of £2,000. The winter season's losses ranged from £100 to £130 per week.

New attractions in 1903 included demonstrations of the Armore Wireless System, transmitting between the Palace and Paris and which 'experts' confidently predicted to be a novelty which would fail, while the construction of Dr Barton's airship brought many to his shed, provided and funded by the Trustees, funds they hoped to recoup from gate money, while Texan aeronaut S.F. Cody built his newly invented war kites in the old Banqueting Hall. There were few other reasons to visit. Newspapers described 'the desolate park waste and tottering building' or 'the long, tortuous climb from Wood Green station', calling the approach from Muswell Hill to the terraces a 'disgrace'.

A letter in the *Finchley Press & Muswell Hill Mercury* of 9 January 1904 alleged: 'We hear that the building is dangerous, we can see it is shockingly neglected and as to the grounds, they are simply a wilderness of decay, desolation and quagmire: no paths, no seats, no flowers, no lamps and no policemen'. The writer continued: 'racecourse and catering income is squandered on unnecessary salaries to an unnecessary crowd of officials and hangers on'.

The Sentinel of 22 January announced a necessary reduction in winter expenses. The manager resigned, with the secretary taking on this additional role. The Palace and Park were to close at dusk, except for visitors to the skating rink. The Great Hall and other parts of the Palace would be available for concerts and meetings with occasional oratorios on Saturday evenings, The Palace would be open from 1.00 to 3.00 p.m. on Sundays but Sunday afternoon concerts would be suspended. Expenditure would be reduced by approximately £137 per week. The *Tottenham Times* of 6 May announced that: 'Happily, there is reason to believe that the bad days of the Palace are over'.

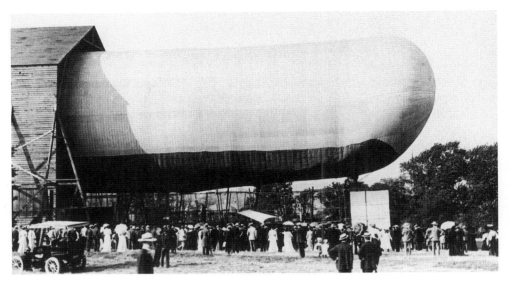

Crowds flocking to see Dr Barton's airship.

The *Daily News* of 6 June 1904 reported a speech by Winston Churchill in the Great Hall. Because of poor acoustics listeners made ear trumpets from their programmes and by the time Winston Churchill spoke there was a forest of little paper megaphones directed towards the platform from the outskirts of the audience.

The *Daily Telegraph* of 1 August wrote of the good weather and crowds (estimated to be about 60,000) adding: '...but except on holiday occasions when the weather is favourable, there is little evidence from the state of the grounds and buildings that the public is seconding the efforts of the Trustees'. The *North Middlesex Chronicle* of 13 August described the Park as: 'very untidy, dejected and sadly neglected. Men are cutting the grass for haymaking. Why are the Trustees not selling the hay?'

The *Morning Leader* of 10 September reported that over 200 men were employed in laying the sewers to carry away the water for the new tram tracks. The *Morning Advertiser* and *The Star* of 14 September both confirmed the story, predicting the trams would be ready for spring.

The *Hornsey Journal* of 8 October added that although currently inconvenient, shortly there would be excellent paths and roads, together with electric trams and light railways which would bring people from all over London to the doors of the Palace.

The *Standard* of 29 November described the glass roof of the Great Hall as unsafe and leaking, and taking at least £4,000 to be repaired. Work on this and the Industrial Hall had begun but was then abandoned from lack of funds:

> The Exhibition Hall, covered in glass from top to bottom and the two great domes flanking the east and west of the building are all in disrepair, as is the large conservatory at one end of the Palace. The barn-like theatre needs repair and restoration. From floor to roof the whole of the Palace is in a discreditable state.

Above: *Firework display.* Below: *The fairground.*

The approaches to the Park are deplorable. The pathway leading from the Grove entrance at Muswell Hill to the Palace is an eyesore. The Priory entrance, at the Hornsey end of the grounds is so dangerous that vehicular traffic has been prohibited. This is having an appreciable effect on revenue. If the roads were in fit condition for carriages it is anticipated many of the more well-to-do classes, who prefer this mode of reaching the Palace, would be among the visitors. The paths leading from Wood Green to Muswell Hill and to Hornsey remain untouched, and when the earth is sodden, as now, they form a perfect quagmire. There are no fewer than twelve glasshouses in the grounds, each 150ft in length. Six have been repaired, but the remaining glass roofs have fallen in and the houses are useless. The fence surrounding the Park is gradually rotting away.

Long Tom Gun, Easter, 1905.

Dr Barton and his airship – before the first (and last) flight, 1905.

The *North Middlesex Chronicle* of 17 December reported the centre track of the light railway was completed.

In January 1905 unemployed men began renovating the Palace and Park. Lack of funds meant wages would come from public subscriptions. As money arrived slowly, only three full days in work were available for each man. Work was from 8.00 a.m. to 4.00 p.m. and the following week another group of men succeeded them. Married men with large families were given preference.

The *Holloway Press* of 27 January 1905 reported: 'Many came without a penny in their possession and appetites of two or more day's growth. No less than 100 of the 150 were penniless. Men regarded the seventeen shillings and sixpence received in exchange for their labour as a real godsend'.

The *Islington Gazette* of 2 February 1905 reported gifts of building materials and that the tramway on the east side was completed from the gates to within a few yards of the Palace. Positive comments on the spick and span appearance of the Palace appeared in the press. With the trams running and the building refurbished, the future appeared promising for the Trustees. In October 1905 appeals for public donations began, so the unemployed could work at the Palace during the winter.

Easter Monday's attraction was the Long Tom Gun (used by the Boers at Ladysmith) and President Kruger's veldt sleeping waggon, both lent by the City Corporation. Before being placed in the Industrial Hall the floors were strengthened as the gun weighed over 6 tons.

Aeronautical events drew the crowds. On the afternoon of 22 July 1905 Dr Barton made his first, and only, airship ascent. A spectator said: 'The ill fated and much talked about Barton airship made its ascent from the grounds only to descend in a field at Havering near Romford to become a wreck with no further call for its services'. The crew comprised M. Gaudron, Dr Barton, Mr Ranson and Mr Henry Spencer. The Trustees charged for admission to the Park to view the ascent, their percentage being £123 10s 8d. However, the construction of the airship shed had cost the Trustees £450 17s, resulting in a loss of about £327.

The *North Middlesex Chronicle* of 3 March 1906 describes work undertaken by the unemployed. Having no money for materials, eight worthless old boilers were removed from the basement for the bricks to be cleaned and reused. The 'blue-blooded residents in the Great Hall had received the attentions of the painter and now looked presentable if not royal. Their condition last year can only be described as shameful. They looked like out-of-works'.

The Trustees announced that, rather than sack them, the wages of attendants and park keepers were reduced by between 2-3s per week, Meanwhile, the demolition of Dr Barton's airship shed began and the old circus ring, last used as a cattle byre and described as a 'sadly dilapidated landmark' was handed over to housebreakers.

In May 1907 The *North Middlesex Chronicle* described the catering as 'cold tea, hard rolls and microscopic pats of butter', with eighty pats of butter now expected from a pound.

The annual meeting of the Palace Trustees in June 1907 was a gloomy event indeed. Newspapers reported on the bad and dangerous state of the building and grounds through lack of money. Replying to a question, Secretary Mr Goodship said the estimated price for all the necessary work to be done was about £25-30,000.

The *Hornsey Journal* of 10 August 1907 reported that if the racecourse lease was not renewed in 1909 the Trustees would lose an annual sum of £4,000 for no outlay. Weekday attractions continued to flop, while the fairground and other entertainments drew crowds only at weekends and on bank holidays.

In January 1908 the newspapers referred to the unemployed men and their families reduced to starvation for want of work. By February over 200 men were working in the Palace and grounds. Matters were not helped by a flu epidemic in February and March. The Trustees provided a canteen where substantial meals cost 5d with other refreshments at low prices. In March 1908 a concert was held for money to repair the Palace – a sum of £2,000 was needed. In June Henry Burt appealed to nine thousand influential persons in the City of London for money to give work to the unemployed at the Palace. The response was insufficient to cover the appeal's postage of £10.

By the end of 1908 matters had worsened. Because of the Trustees' inability to borrow money they had a capital debt of nearly £9,000 which could not be liquidated. Wages were cut and staff laid off. On 2 January 1909 the circus performers went on strike, despite having a large waiting audience. The same occurred the following week. Owed their wages, they refused to work until the debt was settled.

A Palace visitor in January 1909 wrote to the *North Middlesex Chronicle*, complaining the building was so cold he purchased a cup of coffee for threepence. In an ice cold cup with icy milk the drink was lukewarm. He continued:

> The members of the Lyell Taylor Choir were walking about in overcoats and furs, the bandsmen blew their fingers instead of their trumpets, the strings flapped their arms to keep warm – the audience hammered the floor with their feet to keep the blood flowing and urge the performance to begin.

Another writer to the *North Middlesex Chronicle* in February described the deserted Palace and poor state of the skating rink and skates, alleging hirers had to repair the skates before whirling around – with no music – as snow blew through the windows onto the skaters below.

'Cock Robin', writing in the *North Middlesex Chronicle* of 5 June said:

> I am glad to hear my old friend the Alexandra Palace has 'turned the corner' once more. Since I have known it the Palace has done little but turn corners … and we have heard so many times that the Trustees are just on the very needlepoint of making it a paying concern, that I am beginning to think it is one of those long lanes that have no turning. The Palace, last year, according to the balance sheet, made a profit of £79.13.5 against a dead loss on the previous year of £615.18.4, so we are getting on.

Celebrations to honour the King's birthday in June carried an admission charge of 1s. The event was described as being quite deserted, there being at one time in the early afternoon almost as many policemen and attendants present as visitors. Yet the entertainment provided – from bands to fireworks – was excellent of its kind. The Trustees were much disappointed at the poor response to their endeavours.

The Cagney loco miniature railway, 1905.

The Protestant Demonstration in July brought even more woes. The *North Middlesex Chronicle* reported that 'the engine man who had charge of the organ blowing apparatus is said to be a Roman Catholic. At any rate he struck work and let the fire out so that after the first piece or two the organ failed till the evening, by which time the authorities had replaced the man with one who was not anti-Protestant'. The *Daily Express* of 19 July added: 'Just as their concert was beginning the organ, said to be the finest in the world, gave out with a wail and it was discovered that all the fires had been drawn out and all the steam pipes opened on which it [the organ] depends for the working of its bellows'. The *Musical Herald* of August 1909 reported that the person responsible had been dismissed.

Rarely out of the news, the Palace's press coverage was usually negative. In July, a correspondent identified only as 'P.P.' grumbled to the *Hornsey Journal* about the unwholesome, primitive lavatories while the *Islington Gazette* of 20 October 1909 complained of the Palace's unlit approaches. Christmas brought no relief from the Palace's troubles. The seasonal entertainment was described as being 'very poor' while attendance was 'sparse'.

A remarkable event occurred on Guy Fawkes Night 1910. A choral performance of Mackenzie's *Rose of Sharon* in the Great Hall was disrupted by rockets and showers of sparks coming through holes in the roof.

The *Holloway Press* of 13 May 1911 reported the opening of tennis courts at the Palace. Alderman Sloper of the Trustees announced in June that debt was slowly reducing and predicted the Palace would be solvent by 1914. Unlike his fellow Trustees the press were kinder to him, and frequent stories were aired about his dedication to the Palace. Many related how he was at the Palace day and night, sweeping floors, tidying up or doing repairs. Concerns were expressed about his domestic life and health.

Pierrot show in the Japanese village.

Festivities celebrating the Coronation of King George V and Queen Mary in June included the Mayor's Fête to honour this event. Princess Helena (the fifth child of Queen Victoria), the Princess Christian of Schleswig-Holstein, visited the Palace on 3 July, scandalising onlookers by arriving in a motor car rather than horse and carriage. Among the crowds were 410 specially invited old age pensioners who dined on roast beef, lamb and mint sauce, roast chicken, York ham, pressed beef, hot peas, potatoes, salads, tomatoes, butter and biscuits, fruit tarts and jellies, ale, ginger beer and lemonade for abstainers. The meal was described as being 'hugely enjoyed, with many toasts in a fervent manner' to the mayor and mayoress. Later came supper plus gifts, each woman receiving a quarter pound of tea, with a briar pipe for every man.

On 9 September 1911, the *North Middlesex Chronicle* announced that another £500 of debt on the building has been repaid. The newspaper added: 'When Alderman Sloper prophesied that the Palace would eventually be free of debt, he was looked upon as a gentleman who should be put under some form of restraint, but now even the most pessimistic of pessimists has to admit that the Palace's finances are well on the road to where debt ends and prosperity begins'.

Part of this reversal in the Palace's fortunes was attributed to the trams which began running through the Park to the Palace in 1905 and 1906. Mostly the trams were under-utilised, only when the Palace was holding a special weekend or on bank holidays were they crowded to capacity, generating much grumbling from irate passengers.

Above, left: *Balloon ascent, August bank holiday Monday, 1903.*
Above, right: *Balloonist Dolly Shepherd making an impromptu ascent by balloon wearing a long dress and ordinary shoes, 1911/12.*
Below: *The audience appears more interested in the camera than the balloon.*

Whatever attractions the Palace offered, people often chose to spend their rare leisure time on other diversions, including charabanc rides to the country and seaside, visiting Southend by paddle steamer or train, while nearer home music halls and public houses vied for business. Firework displays, balloon and parachute ascents and descents continued to be successful Palace attractions but, as always, the crowds congregated more outside the Palace's perimeter rather than enter and spend money. Balloonists were always popular, mostly for the prospect of their crashing or coming to a sticky end in mid-air, rather than for their skills. A Palace favourite, the ubiquitous balloonist Professor Baldwin died in 1905 by blowing himself up while airborne but, disobligingly for loyal spectators, not at the Palace.

At a special meeting of the Executive Committee on 16 April 1912, it was agreed the Trustees should run the catering, thus ensuring that all profits accrued to the Palace rather than to the catering management who, until this change, passed on only a percentage of profits. Trustees Sloper and Barfield undertook negotiations with the caterers and suppliers of beers and spirits, reorganising not only the food but bar tariffs as well.

Cost-cutting included examining the entertainments and making changes to benefit the Palace rather than the entertainments' proprietors.

By December 1912 at a meeting of Haringey Burgesses it was announced that the Palace's debt was now below £3,000 with a great improvement in the catering since being run by the Palace. In May 1913 Alderman Sloper, at a meeting of the Trustees, announced that profits were the best ever, with those on catering showing a surplus of £600, of which £500 had gone to pay off a loan from the Union of London and Smith's Bank. Also, for the first time the theatre had made a profit while the cinematograph had really gripped the public's imagination. The Alderman's prophecy of solvency by 1914 no longer appeared foolishly optimistic.

Indeed, at the annual meeting of the Trustees in May 1914, Alderman Sloper, his prophecy of solvency vindicated, announced a surplus of income over expenditure of £2,156.

On 5 August 1914 Britain went to war with Germany.

✣ THREE ✣

IN THE BEGINNING

On the evening of bank holiday Monday, 3 August 1914, William Beveridge of the Board of Trade wrote to his mother: 'London sights and streets have ... been very strange. All day today the crowds have been thick – standing in the roadway, sitting on the railings opposite the Houses of Parliament and sitting in tiers on the base of Nelson's Column'. Tuesday 4 August 1914 had dawned to brilliant sunshine. In London, crowds in a state of feverish excitement were everywhere, many waving union jacks and tricolours, singing Rule Britannia, the Marseillaise and The Red, White and Blue. With the future of Europe in the balance, war was on everyone's mind and the only word on their lips since 28 July, when First Sea Lord Winston Churchill had given orders for the Navy to head for their war base at Scapa Flow.

A mood of war euphoria consumed the British population. 'One could not stay in the house ... there was a feeling of an inner smouldering which at moments bursts into intense excitement... Crowds of people were in the streets' wrote Mrs C.S. Peel in *How We Lived Then*.

Poet and essayist Humbert Wolfe, an observer of the London scene that night, later wrote: '...we watched the mob go roaring and cheering past brandishing flags'.

In the early evening the King signed a proclamation of army mobilisation, Thousands thronged Buckingham Palace, calling for the King. Mrs Peel wrote: 'The red geraniums outside Buckingham Palace looked redder than they had ever looked before. The Palace, seen against the sky, appeared as if cut out of steel. It seemed as if inanimate things might suddenly become alive and do something'.

The Times correspondent Michael McDonagh, writing in *London during the Great War* described the scene: 'During the evening the King and Royal family appeared on the balcony on three separate occasions, the King wearing the uniform of an Admiral of the Fleet, because the chanting of the crowd slowly and with emphasis, betokening that they would have no refusal, "We – want – our – King". His Majesty smiled and bowed, bowed and smiled, while the throng sang to him that he was a jolly good fellow, again, again and again'.

Later that evening, while watching the feverishly excited crowds from his office windows and the city's lights twinkling in the dusk, Foreign Secretary Sir Edward Grey is recorded as saying to a friend: 'The lamps are going out all over Europe: we shall not see them lit again in our lifetime'.

The area around Downing Street and Parliament Square was packed as Big Ben chimed its eleven hours. As the final stroke died away – signifying the start of hostilities, the crowds swarming in Downing Street, Parliament Street and Parliament Square, burst with one accord into 'God Save the King'. Despite there being no official announcement or proclamation of war the crowd then scattered in all directions, running and shouting 'War! War! War!' as they dispersed.

In Whitehall, just after midnight, the telegraph operator sent the signing off signal along the one remaining cable to Berlin – GN (Good Night). This line would stay dead for more than four years.

'BRITAIN AT WAR!' proclaimed *The Times* placards in bold black print on 5 August. In the Commons Prime Minister Asquith announced to a packed House: 'Since eleven o'clock last night a state of war has existed between this country and Germany'. Later, Chancellor of the Exchequer, Lloyd George, told the House that gold coinage would be withdrawn from circulation and used as a munition of war. The Government had decided to issue Treasury notes of 20s and 10s value – 3million by Friday, and afterwards at the rate of 5million a day until the supply was considered sufficient.

The Aliens Restriction Act was passed on 5 August, going through Parliament almost unchallenged. This Act gave the Government *carte blanche* in matters relating to aliens, thus enabling 'His Majesty in time of war or imminent danger of great emergency by order in council to impose restrictions on aliens and make such provisions as appear necessary or expedient for carrying such restrictions into effect'. Home Secretary Reginald McKenna assured the House that '…the legislation would continue in effect only as long as the war or "a state of national danger or grave emergency" exists'. He went on to say that 'the Government intended to cause as little inconvenience as possible to friendly aliens. Alien enemies, against whom there is no reason whatever to suppose that they are engaged in operations against this country will be subjected to nothing further than registration and provisions that they may not live in prohibited areas'.

The Times of 6 August reported that Mr McKenna's speech was interrupted by cheers and, during a reference to the arrest of spies, one MP called that 'they ought to be shot'. Early that morning, Post Office engineers had severed the Anglo–German cables below the low-water mark. At Dover, a cable ship which had been on standby went to sea to cut the German cables to Brest, Vigo, Tenerife and New York.

As the Army had only eighty motor vehicles and 25,000 horses at the outbreak of war, horses for transport were commandeered from carts and carriages, soon filling parks, fields and even the moat at the Tower of London. Assisted by police officers, Army buyers snapped up horses and motor vehicles from private individuals, showrooms and manufacturers, wagons and buses were taken, repainted and sent for the war effort, while commercial vans were utilised as troop transporters and goods carriers. Scotland Yard was busy; it had begun rounding up and imprisoning known and suspected German agents, while armourers, under the rules of mobilisation, set to work sharpening officers' swords, making them ready for battle. Britain was buzzing.

Immediately panic buying of food began. Queues of well-dressed, comfortably-off women soon formed outside provision shops, some of which closed in the early afternoon, their shelves bare. Banks remained closed to prevent a run on savings and investments with a moratorium declared on debt settlement.

'Your King and Country needs YOU' was the message on the first recruitment posters which appeared on Thursday 6 August. In vivid blue letters on a white background and bordered in red, the poster demanded unmarried men between the ages of eighteen and thirty to rally round the flag and enlist in the ranks of the Army. Another, headed 'A Call

Right: Daily Graphic, *5 August 1914*
– announcing outbreak of war.

Below: Daily Graphic, *5 August 1914*
– reassurances to readers regarding food supplies.

BREAD AND MEAT IN ABUNDANCE.

SPLENDID FOOD REPORT BY CABINET COMMITTEE.

ALL FEARS GROUNDLESS.

THREAT TO MANUFACTURED RISES IN PRICE.

There are abundant supplies of wheat and of meat in this country. There is no occasion for any rise in food prices.

This is the official statement of the Cabinet Committee.

We are officially informed by the Home Office that the Committee of the Cabinet appointed to deal with food supplies consider it necessary to issue an immediate statement for the information of the public as to the actual position. The President of the Board of Agriculture has already stated that the supply of wheat at present in the country, together with the home crops now being harvested, is sufficient for four months' ordinary consumption. In this statement no account is taken of wheat at this moment on the sea or to be shipped. Large consignments of wheat are now on the way to this country, and much of it is, in fact, close to our shores.

AT WAR WITH GERMANY.

SUMMARY REJECTION OF ULTIMATUM.

DECLARATION BY GREAT BRITAIN.

GERMAN ACTION.

INVASION & FIGHTING IN BELGIUM BEGUN.

SEA AND LAND BATTLES.

Above, left: *Anti-German propaganda, 1914.*

Above, right: *Poster for the British Empire Union, c. 1914.*

Left: *Cartoon in* Modern Life, *31 October 1914.*

to Arms' said: 'An addition of 100,000 men to His Majesty's Regular Army is immediately necessary in the present grave national emergency'. This enormous figure, demanded by newly appointed War Minister Lord Kitchener, was greeted by both government and public with disbelief – everyone knew the war would be over by Christmas. However, veteran military campaigner Lord Kitchener thought otherwise, already fearing that the 100,000 men demanded would be insufficient. The thousands of young men who had been clamouring for war responded immediately. Michael McDonagh, correspondent for *The Times*, wrote: 'The recruiting headquarters is in Old Scotland Yard, off Whitehall. As I passed there this evening I saw a big throng of young men still in straw hats, waiting their turn to get in and, in the old phrase, "take the King's shilling"'.

On Friday 7 August, while the country was still coming to terms with being on a war footing, in Parliament the Defence of the Realm Act (DORA) was rushed through so fast that it was not even printed. Home Secretary McKenna presented to the House a brief handwritten draft of some of the Act's provisions. McKenna asked the House for leave to bring in 'a Bill to make Regulations during the present war for the defence of the Realm'. DORA had been specifically designed (a) to prevent persons communicating with the enemy or obtaining information for that purpose or any purpose calculated to jeopardise the success of the operations of any of His Majesty's forces or to assist the enemy and (b) to secure the safety of any means of communication, or of railways, docks or harbours. This incomplete statute (which over the coming years would give governments unlimited powers to impinge on all areas of British life), gave the government virtual powers of martial law, to make sweeping decisions, take rapid action and suspend individual rights. In the course of the war the Act also empowered the government to take state control of the railways for the transport of munitions, materials and troops.

Leave having been given, the Bill was brought in by the Home Secretary and read for a first time. It was then ordered to be printed. It was run through Committee, reported to the House, read a third time and passed. All this was done to the accompaniment of loud cheers. The House had recovered its voice.

A sense of urgency and excitement swept throughout the country. Trains were commandeered to move the army and were soon filled with soldiers travelling to the coast. Many of the carriages bore the chalked legend 'Next stop Berlin'. Recruitment exceeded expectations, and many towns and villages soon formed their own battalions of Pals. Elderly policemen and Army reservists were called out of retirement to do their bit.

Seaports were busy with ships carrying Britons and Americans returning from Europe, while on their outward journeys they were filled with returning German and Austro-Hungarian citizens and their families. Many carried men returning to enlist in the armies of their homelands.

Food hoarding, spies, tales of British military disasters on land and sea – anything was believed, no matter how dubious a story's provenance. The fact that newspapers did not publish these stories did not prove them untrue, but was regarded as proof that newspapers were being 'muzzled by the Government'. Within this mêlée, whipped up by the press and publications such as *John Bull*, the many Germans and Austrians who regarded Britain as their home and with little or no connection to Europe, soon found themselves unemployed, destitute and homeless. As August was a warm, dry month many single men slept in parks but when the autumn rains set in, these people suffered. Although many had been with the same employer for years, married German, Austrian and Hungarian men with families were immediately dismissed from their jobs and evicted from their homes, frequently only one or two rented rooms. The Religious Society of Friends (Quakers) in Great Britain arranged a soup kitchen and tried to help the men and their families in a variety of ways, including the granting of small cash sums. By November 1914 the Quakers had dealt with nearly 3,000 cases, including an invalid German Baron to a little Hungarian dwarf on the music hall stage who had been sent back to the German frontier, where he hoped to earn money for his fare home.

Part of a report dated 12 September 1914 by the Quaker Emergency Committee for Assistance of Germans, Austrians and Hungarians in Distress read:

> ...there are hundreds of distressing cases of aliens who cannot, or would not, leave the country. Many of the women are English who have become aliens by marriage. Numbers of distressed waiters have been helped over the past few weeks ... but most of them are now being taken off to military camps by the War Office ... their families are dependent upon private charity or the workhouse.

Under the Aliens Restriction Act, people of German origin were required to register with the police in the district where they lived by 17 August. *The Manchester Guardian* of 10 August 1914 reported the scene outside the police station in Tottenham Court Road: where the queue comprised many quiet looking old ladies, probably teachers; young German girl students; tourists caught without money; barbers; stockbrokers; shipping clerks; waiters; bankers and some of the less reputable occupations'. Failure to register attracted a fine of £100 or six months' imprisonment. Language difficulties often meant people had to wait hours before being seen.

The *Police Review and Parade Gossip* of 14 August reported officers working twelve hour days as at the beginning of registration there were more than one thousand persons daily waiting to register and many of those registering had not visited their home country for more than fifty years and professed themselves more British than the English. The paper also reported a rush of householders at police stations who had suddenly become suspicious of their German neighbours, or who had a German subject living with them.

Britain declared war on Germany's ally, the Austro-Hungarian Empire, on 12 August, thus giving Austrians and Hungarians until 24 August to register. On 13 August nearly 2,000 aliens from all three countries were interned in what was to be the first of the many 'sweeps' by the police which would take place over the coming months. *The Times* of 17 August reported that on the previous evening the Austrian Ambassador, Count Mensdorff, had left Paddington station. While being seen off by Foreign Office officials some forty Germans on another platform began singing *Deutschland Uber Alles*. Britons also on the platforms began to sing *God Save the King*. Both sides sang louder and louder to drown each other out.

❧ FOUR ❧

ALLY PALLY

The thousands that flocked to Alexandra Palace on bank holiday Monday, 3 August 1914, had, like everyone in Britain, the threat of war on their minds. The gloomy morning weather did not deter people from making the most of the last bank holiday before Christmas or, indeed, possibly the last for some time.

A lunchtime storm brought a sunny afternoon whose stiff breeze sent many into the Palace building to enjoy the indoor entertainment. The cinema and roller-skating rink were crowded, as was the organ recital in the Great Hall, while a massed band played selections of patriotic music interspersed with variety entertainment. Outside, hardier souls braving the winds that always play around the Palace on its northern heights, kept the fairground, boating lake and switchback busy while others enjoyed dancing the waltz, two step and variety tango to the Palace orchestra playing in the Grove. Despite the air of merriment, many groups were in deep discussion on the looming European crisis.

Some of the day's advertised attractions had been cancelled. Spencer Bros had planned a balloon ascent from the Palace's South Front: this was stopped by the War Office and Home Secretary, who had forbidden all flying. Another casualty was 'Little Mary', whose act comprised balancing on a large globe of the world. Performing on the Continent, Little Mary's globe had aroused such suspicion that she and the globe were detained in Berlin while customs authorities searched them thoroughly.

As darkness fell, the Palace's day closed with a massive firework display which culminated in a shower of rockets and a patriotic set piece. Whether the pyrotechnics lightened the hearts of the home-going public is debatable. Probably most had their minds on the following day and the outcome of Britain's ultimatum to Germany not to invade Belgium.

'Until further notice the Palace grounds are closed to the public, who are warned that any unauthorised person found in the grounds is liable to be shot. BY ORDER.'

This poster greeted visitors to Alexandra Palace in the first days of war. The message was reinforced by locked gates and armed sentries patrolling the grounds. Along with all the gossip about spies and sabotage, rumours on the wartime future of the Palace immediately sprang to life. Newspapers of 11 August informed their readers that they had it on the 'best authority' that a wealthy and well-known London businessman proposed fitting out the Palace at his own expense for those who would be 'broken in the war' but for now they were sworn to secrecy. Other stories insisted the Palace would be used as an aerial station or as a military camp for prisoners of war. Word soon spread and the weekend saw large crowds thronging the Palace gates, gazing at the notice as if fascinated by the idea that if one of them climbed over the fence a shot might ring out.

The *Wood Green Sentinel* of 14 August wrote:

> One of the local surprises brought about by the war has been the closing of the Alexandra Palace and grounds to the public. When the Palace staff left at midnight on Friday last they had no idea that the accommodation of the military would mean that the public would not be admitted. Indeed, some gain to the Trustees was looked for from the public desire to "see the soldiers" as at Jubilee time. But on Saturday morning they found the place in the possession of the military and a notice on the gate that "all unauthorised persons" found in the Palace would be liable to be shot! An Act of Parliament made the Palace free for the public's enjoyment "for ever" but Civil Law goes by the board in wartime. We now have to prevent the Germans of possessing themselves of it. That's something of our very own to fight for!

In view of the spy mania sweeping the country, the following news item in the *Wood Green Weekly Herald* of 15 August, was not surprising: 'Two men of foreign appearance were detained by the police at Alexandra Palace on Thursday evening on suspicion of being German spies. It later transpired that one was a Russian who had been in business in London for over thirty years and the other was a Jew. Both were liberated after establishing their identities.'

The *Middlesex Chronicle* of the same date stated: 'I have heard it is suggested that the Palace may be used for keeping prisoners of war and we may yet see a modern von Moltke or Bismarck looking out from that police station at the centre of the racecourse. It would be an ideal situation and if any emperors are captured, they could hardly grumble at a suite of rooms in a real palace with a queen's name.'

Unknown to the public, at the meeting of the Alexandra Palace Executive Committee of 28 July 1914, it was agreed that the Committee reply to a letter requesting space for soldiers and their horses to be billeted at the Palace in the event of mobilisation. The first wartime occupants of the Palace were cavalry – King Edward's Own Light Horse – also known as the King's Overseas Dominion Regiment. Composed of gentlemen of colonial birth or those who had seen service in the colonies, this elite corps (or Swagger Regiment) was based at Chelsea and the only special reserve cavalry regiment in England. Created at the time of the Boer War, in which it served with distinction, at full muster the regiment numbered nearly 500 who, together with their horses, occupied part of the Palace and grounds. They were a popular sight; denied access to the Palace, visitors crowded outside the railings of the Avenue Lawn Tennis Club to view the horses picketed there. Some horses were hunters while others had been taken from pulling carts, so included many new to the work, and who were unused to being tethered in the open. On the Thursday night of their stay the horses stampeded, resulting in the destruction of a large part of the Palace grounds and the injury and death of several horses.

The troops did not linger at the Palace. On the second Sunday of their stay a religious service was held before the first contingent moved out, the second leaving on Monday. A reporter from the *Holloway Press* of 21 August attended the ceremony and wrote:

> I managed to make my way inside the grounds and was privileged to witness a service in the Great Hall. The men, clad in their uniforms of grey with red facings, only filled the first few rows of the chairs, and the clergyman addressed them from the centre of the platform where the conductor stands for the massed band concerts. It was very impressive, and although the empty hall gave back the speaker's voice in echo upon echo one could not but feel the solemnity of the occasion. One felt that these men were going on active service at the call of duty and it might well be that many of them would not return. Then, as their full throated voices gave forth the grand hymn 'Onward Christian Soldiers' and the vaulted roof repeated the refrain, one forgot the bare, almost deserted Palace, and understood.
>
> After the service one squadron departed, the other two leaving on Monday, all for a secret destination. By 2.00 p.m. the Palace had reopened to the public and the few visitors were surprised to see all signs of military occupation removed. The Palace Trustees announced there were no further plans for the Palace to be used in connection with the war at present.

Local newspapers reported that entertainment would take place as usual on the weekend of 22-23 August. On Saturday night, Mr J.C. Parker would conduct the Palace Orchestra on the bandstand in the Grove, accompanying vocalists Miss Patricia Plowman and Mr Walter Montague. Sunday promised that Mr G.D. Cunningham would give his usual organ recital in the Great Hall. The evening concert would be provided by the popular Palladium Orchestra, plus Miss Carrie Lancely and Mr Ceredig Walters. Also, some good pictures were due to be shown.

The Thursday evening dances and concerts would also be resumed, and the roller-skating rink and picture theatre had reopened. A full programme was advertised for the last weekend of August. This included dancing in the Grove to the Palace Orchestra with vocalists Miss Florence Mellors and Mr Walter Kingsley. Sunday's organ recital promised the services of Mr R.G. Thalben-Ball, while the Grove had the Orchestra again, this time with vocalists Miss Lilian Goodison and Mr Gwynn Davies. The cinema had two shows of motion pictures.

Part of a report in the *Hornsey Journal* of 29 August, headed 'Alexandra Palace Trustees', read: 'Owing to the requirements of military duty, nearly all the bands engaged for concerts in the near future have had to cancel their engagements. It is trusted that during the war the public would extend to the Palace the same patronage as they had always done during times of peace'.

Alderman Edwin Sloper added that the Trustees would be grateful to hear that the Colonel and Adjutant of King Edward's horse had written thanking the Trustees for all they had done to make the men comfortable. The Trustees were glad to have been of some little assistance at this time of crisis.

Behind the scenes the mood was not so emollient or patriotic. At a meeting of the Trustees' Executive Committee on 29 August, the minutes recorded that the Avenue Lawn Tennis Club had written to the Trustees regarding damage done to the tennis courts by the troops during their stay. The Trustees informed the Lawn Tennis Club that they must make their own claim to the War Office. The minutes went on to record that the Trustees would also be contacting the War Office to claim compensation for the loss of income during the closure of the Palace, the amount of the claim being based on the takings for the same period in the previous year.

Unaware of this internal friction, on Saturday 5 September, the public were invited to enjoy the Orchestra playing in the illuminated Grove, with Miss Doris Smerdon providing vocals and Mr Charles Wreford his humour. Sunday offered Mr Cunningham on the organ and the Palace Orchestra in the Grove, this time supported by the singing skills of Miss Ethel Kemish and Mr Herbert Carter.

A snippet in *The Queen* for 5 September quoted Mr Edmund Burke, the bass vocalist from Paris: 'At night from my windows I can see the powerful searchlights near the Eiffel Tower scouring the heavens for German Zeppelins or aeroplanes. One hears no music in Paris, no people practising, no orchestras practising. It is depressingly dull'.

The Queen concluded tartly that 'Mr Burke is evidently optimistic, for he expects to sing at Cardiff and the Alexandra Palace in October'.

The Stage of 10 September, reporting on the week's entertainment by Ye Merry Wags described them as giving 'a diversified programme which is calculated to please everybody.' Miss Doris Skipp made a big hit with her sand and mat dance, Miss Winonah Melbourne's dainty manner had a strong appeal, with droll comedian Mr Harry Hughes, ventriloquist and conjurer Mr Darrel Yorke, while Mr Harry Hughes gives a good living marionette show'. The following week promised The Grey Dons. They never arrived; the Palace closed to the public on Friday 11 September 1914.

❧ FIVE ❧

FRIENDS AND ENEMIES

In August the war appeared to be progressing in Britain's favour. The British Expeditionary Force of 70,000 men landed in France on the 17th – the Russians being defeated at the Battle of Tannenberg and the Austrians at Lemberg, while at the Battle of the Marne, British and French troops were advancing. Prophecies of the war being over by Christmas no longer seemed far-fetched. However, the Battle of Mons on 23 August, the first formal engagement between the British and German forces, saw the British defeated and withdrawing to Picardy. About 300 lightly wounded officers and men, the first British casualties, arrived at Waterloo station a few days later. They were transported to hospital in Lyons' Teashop delivery vans, as there were insufficient ambulances. At the same time the first influx of Belgian refugees were arriving.

Before the Palace's closure to the public, the Trustees had been approached by the Local Government Board (LGB). On 11 September the Metropolitan Asylum Board (MAB) took over the Palace, supervised by Dr Herbert Cuff, Principal Medical Officer of the MAB at an agreed weekly rent of £250; this sum included coal to the value of no more than £20 weekly, plus the use of the Palace's catering staff. By 14 September 1,000 beds had been installed, while by the end of that week the number of beds had risen to 3,000 and the first 500 Belgians had been welcomed to their temporary home. By the end of October over 19,000 refugees had been admitted then passed on to permanent accommodation.

By the beginning of September North London newspapers already carried stories of arrests involving German and Austrian citizens, many of whom had been resident in Britain for decades. The *Police Review and Parade Gossip* of 11 September reported:

Drastic measures have been begun by the police in London for dealing with the number of 'alien enemies' who now, rapidly becoming destitute, are considered as likely to be a source of danger. At the offices of the German Benevolent Society some three or four hundred Germans daily gather, clamouring for assistance as being out of employment and without means. The majority were young and had the appearance of waiters, kitchen and hotel hands. Those who were registered as married were allowed to go, but eventually it was decided to detain ninety of the 'captures' as being destitute and liable to be a danger to the realm. By 28 August 4,300 enemy aliens had been interned.

The *Wood Green Herald* of 4 September reported a series of charges against local aliens arrested for not registering and other offences. One young German woman was told by the chairman of the bench that regulations had been made to safeguard this country and the only people she had to blame were her own, who had abused British hospitality by coming here and giving away secrets. She was fined 40s and costs; she paid the fine immediately.

Arrested as an alien enemy was Rudolph Schmidt (59), who had lived in Tottenham for eight of the twenty-four years he had resided in England. He was charged with keeping four pigeons on his premises. The birds were produced in court. Detective Forde, while acknowledging he was no expert, believed the pigeons could be used for carrying messages. Mr Schmidt declared he kept the pigeons for killing and eating. Refused bail and remanded in custody, he elected for trial by jury.

This case, and many others involving pigeons, can be traced to the Metropolitan Police Orders of 4 September. Pigeon ownership greatly exercised the constabulary. The *Police Chronicle* of 5 September carried an article entitled 'Pigeons as spies. Birds owned by Germans to be killed' which alleged:

> The authorities intend to confiscate or kill all pigeons owned by alien enemies in this country. This strong action follows upon information supplied to the War Office recently by a pigeon expert. 'The Germans have for years been training pigeons to fly from England' said the editor of the *Racing Pigeon* recently. 'Their government subsidises lofts of pigeons which are kept in various places, including the ports. These pigeons have no doubt been used as spies for many years. A pigeon has flown 600 miles in ten hours. Every effort must be made to kill a bird seen flying across the North Sea. It might be quite as important for the crew of a warship to bring it down as for them to hit an aeroplane.' Since the war detectives have visited a number of lofts and have compelled their German owners to kill their birds. Many birds are worth £10 each.

Unconcerned by such avian agonising, of far greater curiosity to North Londoners were the Belgian residents of Alexandra Palace. The arrival and departure of vans containing beds and other furniture was of constant interest, while the newspapers kept the story going. Crowds gathered outside the Palace railway station to see the new arrivals alighting from trains that had brought them from Harwich, Tilbury and Folkestone. The Germans had entered Brussels on 20 August fomenting tales of German atrocities, so the influx of Belgian refugees to the Palace excited much sympathy. Many local residents hung Belgian and French flags outside their homes as gestures of welcome and solidarity.

The *Moravian Messenger* of 3 October described the refugees:

> From their broken and ravaged homes they have come here for sanctuary from Aerschot and battered Louvain; weak women and sad eyed men, little wide eyed children, wondering why their young lives have been so savagely disturbed. The refugees include about forty nuns from Aerschot, men and women of the peasant class in wooden sabots, old and young in all stations of life. Their homes have been burnt by the Germans, their fields and crops trampled to waste by hordes of soldiers.

Everything possible had been done to welcome the Belgians. Rows of beds packed the Great Hall and other available space. Accommodation was set aside for those of the better classes who were allowed a modicum of privacy in their sleeping arrangements. The theatre was turned into a chapel where the Catholic Belgians could take Mass. The Winter Gardens became a smoking and reading room for the men, children had the freedom of the grounds while the women had been allocated a laundry room to help with the running of the Palace. During wet weather the conservatory was used as a drying area, with lines of washing hanging between the statuary and palm trees. On drier days washing lines erected outside were constantly in use. The Monkey House had been transformed into bathrooms. Despite this latter conversion, the *Wood Green Herald* of 9 October reported that parties of Belgian refugees were taken to the public baths by omnibus as they were badly in need of soap and water. Readers would have been pleased to learn that ablutions were carried out under 'ideal sanitary conditions'.

Laundry drying in the conservatory.

Food and clothing with tobacco for the men poured in. The local newspapers requested that the avalanche of top hats and morning coats be stilled: these garments were deemed unsuitable for the mainly peasant influx. A Muswell Hill milliner, moved by the hatless plight of the women, invited some of them to her shop and fitted them with hats free of charge. However, *The Times* of 29 September described the refugees as follows:

> …women wear neither hat nor bonnet, for with them, as with women of many countries, the shawl is very common and, folded usually across the shoulders, serves as a covering for the head in cold and rainy weather. The peasantry are distinguishable from the urban working class by the wearing of the wooden shoes called sabots, which are so popular with those who labour in the fields. Many of them look as if they had stepped out of Millet's famous pictures *The Sower*, *The Reaper* or *The Angelus*.

Another description of the Belgian refugees portrayed them thus:

> …the main bulk of them obviously were peasants – dark complexioned and undersized, most of them. There were whole families – parents and several young children … the Belgians are very properly the guests of the nation.

On 22 September Queen Mary visited. After spending three-quarters of an hour touring the Palace the Queen made a speech which was translated into Flemish. She departed to cries of 'Vive la Reine!'

Anti-German feeling ran high. Tales of ever more barbaric German atrocities related by the 'brave little Belgians' fuelled the flames. Spy stories were rife. Many knew someone with an unimpeachable reputation for truth who had an apocryphal tale to tell of gun emplacements in German gardens disguised as tennis courts, plus extra deep cellars under houses. Trains were allegedly derailed and signalmen overcome in their boxes, while armed sentries were also attacked by bands of Germans who vanished as inexplicably as they arrived. Mysterious ladies – invariably dressed in grey – signalled messages to the enemy from remote places on the coast, while sinister German governesses had travelling trunks whose false bottoms concealed weapons and explosives. These women either vanished in strange circumstances or were alleged to have been shot in the Tower of London.

The story of an immense army of Russian soldiers was everywhere. Supposedly a million strong, many reported seeing them passing through England on their way to France from Archangel – just before the port was closed by ice – they allegedly landed at Leith then were carried at night to South Coast ports in hundreds of trains with blinds down but still affording glimpses of fierce-looking armed men in fur hats. Stories of railway porters having to remove roubles from slot machines or sweep snow dropped from the Russians' boots at Edinburgh station abounded and, despite denials, the Russians were believed by many to have been a surprise invader in France against the Germans.

While crowds still gathered at Alexandra Palace to see the Belgian arrivals, the first German prisoners of war arrived in England. Described by the newspaper as 'blonde beasts' an eyewitness described them thus: 'The soiled state of the uniforms of all, and their unkempt appearance generally, betokened hardships undergone'. The men were

Above: *Belgian refugees dining in a corridor.* Below: *Belgian refugee men enjoying a smoke.*

transferred to Frith Hill Camp, Frimley, Surrey, after the Battle of the Aisne Salient on 16 September.

Stories of German atrocities continued, ensuring constant agitation against 'the Hun' stayed at boiling point. Many Belgians had a tale to tell. The *Wood Green Herald* of 23 October reported one of many stories related by Belgian refugees. This alleged that seventeen Uhlans (German cavalrymen who carried 12ft long steel lances tipped with a sharpened bayonet) had impaled the head of a seventy-year-old woman on a lance and spiked her two grandchildren with their bayonets.

The same edition reported an anti-German demonstration in Seven Sisters Road, Tottenham. During this, several shops under German ownership were threatened, but few in the 3,000-strong crowd were actively hostile. Local police dispersed the crowd. In a later issue of the paper one of the proprietors – baker Henry C. Kurtz – stressed his loyalty to Britain as a British-born subject, while another, Mr Weiffenbach, who had been in Britain since 1885 and was naturalised, displayed his papers in his shop window. The third victim of the demonstration, butcher Mr C. Spindler, kept his shop closed for a few days.

With the war situation worsening, at the beginning of October public houses were ordered to close at 11.00 p.m. while by the end of the month the first lighting restrictions were imposed: shops were to close early to save lighting and help the blackout. The Royal Navy helped to defend Antwerp, which was soon captured by the Germans, British troops defended the Menin Gate, while 12 October saw the start of First Ypres, which did not end until 11 November. The wearing of mourning black was ever more noticeable.

Meanwhile, the Belgians continued their arrival and departure at Alexandra Palace. Queen Alexandra, the Queen Mother, visited the Palace on 30 October, accompanied by her daughter, the Princess Victoria. Queen Alexandra, visibly moved by the stories of the refugees, promised to send parcels, which eventually arrived.

At the end of October, following the arrival at the Palace of 2,000 French refugees rescued from the mined steamer *Admiral Geautaume* fighting soon broke out between the races. Upon being told they would be returned to France many French absconded, never to be seen again.

Problems had also arisen from the 'good English' treating the 'brave Belgians' to British beer. This was far more potent than Belgian varieties, so it was not long before Belgian names began appearing in the Magistrates' Court list in North London papers. The usual charge was drunk and disorderly. At first, upon hearing the refugees' sad stories and learning of the kindness of their English hosts, magistrates were sympathetic and did not levy punishment, allowing for Belgian misunderstanding of English ways. However, as numbers appearing before them grew, sympathy rapidly died. Soon the Belgians were reported as being fined or sentenced to hard labour, the same as their 'good English' drinking companions. International goodwill also soured among English men, as local newspapers reported fights between the males of the two nations over English women who found Belgian men's continental charms irresistible.

Local newspapers published letters such as that from Tottenham resident Mrs Jessie Herbert of Lansdowne Road, who wrote to the *Wood Green Herald*:

Personally I feel at the present moment that there is no class of people in our midst who can claim our sympathies more than the innocent Germans and Austrians who we compel to remain in our country. They are robbed of their employment, their liberty and their good name, all through no fault of theirs. The Belgians have been robbed of their homes and have suffered much hardship but have not lost their good name and their bravery is rewarded with much sympathy; they can well be proud, but what of the unfortunate Austrians and Germans? I crave for them the sympathy of all broadminded English people and the speedy release from prison of those whose innocence can be proved.

There were two replies to Mrs Herbert's letter in the following week's newspaper. Neither of the respondents, unlike Mrs Herbert, were sufficiently courageous to supply their names or addresses. The first, using the pseudonym 'Justice' responded thus: 'The lady's sympathy would not be ill advised were it devoted to the Belgians who, in addition to the suffering caused by the invaders to innocent civilians, women and children, had the grief of realising that those who lived among them and enjoyed their friendship and hospitality, only awaited an opportunity to betray them', while the second respondent, under the psuedonym 'Penetrant', wrote that:

> The authentication of horrible atrocities, of arrangements long preferred by spies, proves the enemy considers 'all's fair in war' and will do his best to maintain his point of view, the people waging war against us must be treated in such a way that it would be impossible for them to repeat in this country their doings in Belgium where, in numerous instances, Germans who have lived for long periods among us and obtained the confidence of the populace, proved themselves spies during the invasion. She should remember the fact that 'once a German, always a German' and that while seeking our hospitality they naturally appear very innocent and well disposed but they can be, and are, very different when the occasion arises.

John Bull of 14 November reported the account of a private, allegedly with the Durham Light Infantry, who was currently in Britain after being wounded in France. The private had seen the Germans retreating from the Marne and had marched with his regiment through villages which the Germans had hastily abandoned. In one, the private claimed he had seen 'something in a cottage window looking like a grotesque ornament. It was actually a real baby, naked and dead. Perhaps six to eight months old, stuck on a bayonet on the end of a German rifle'.

John Bull asserted that the honest fellow could find no words to express his horror. However, *John Bull* found plenty, ranting that 'for these abominations there must be reprisals, not in kind but according to the utmost severity of our own law. In the end the clean handed vengeance of Britain shall prove more frightful than all the bloody debaucheries of the Berlin slaughter men'.

A favourite theme of *John Bull* was that of interning naturalised Germans who were, of course, spies. The paper alleged that Germans chose to occupy the hillier parts of London purely for the nefarious trade of spying and preparing the ground for an invasion of German military. Any foreigner residing in the heights of Sydenham, Hampstead, Hendon, Highgate, Muswell Hill or the area surrounding Alexandra Palace should be treated with the greatest suspicion. *John Bull* urged its readers to note any tennis courts or light buildings that could be used and dismantled as a base for heavy German artillery after the invasion.

A calmer, balanced view on the 'spy menace' was offered by 'A Detective' in the *Police Review and Parade Gossip* of 13 November. He wrote:

> What is a spy? The answer of the man in the streets is a German, his wife, his family and the whole lot of them. The information obtained by some innocent German bricklayer's

labourer, who cannot speak the language and who is absolutely without a friend in Germany and believes that Leipzig is in France, cannot be of importance, and he is far better out of the internment camp than certain newspaper editors. But he is a German, and a German must be a spy, according to public opinion. I quite agree with the restrictions as regards prohibited areas, but to intern a man who has resided for twenty years in, for instance, Buxton, is panic logic with a vengeance. I am satisfied that greater vigilance will do more to stop espionage than the arrest of any number of respectable German residents in our midst, most of whom are refugees from a country whose militarism has been responsible for their exile to this country, which they believed at the time would be a free haven of refuge and liberty.

The many Germans who came into the category described by 'A Detective' faced a future filled with despair. Matters were not helped by the bombardment of Scarborough, Whitby and Hartlepool on 16 December 1914, the first raid on Britain since 1665. A German air raid on Dover on Christmas Eve caused public outrage. The Germans, unemployed, often homeless, dependent upon small handouts from charities and pariahs in English communities that had been their homes for years, faced the first Christmas of the war with foreboding.

Meanwhile, at Alexandra Palace, the Belgian refugees were celebrating Christmas in grand style. Because of the holiday, relocating the refugees came to a halt. With over 2,000 Belgians at the Palace both locals and the Trustees gave their time and gifts to make the holiday memorable. A large Christmas tree, draped with over £100-worth of presents was erected in the Great Hall, dwarfing Alderman Sloper who, dressed as Father Christmas and with more presents pinned to his outfit, danced around with the children and led them to the Lucky Dip. Smaller trees were erected and decorated in other parts of the Palace. Among the entertainments for the adults Mr G.D. Cunningham gave an organ recital in the Great Hall. This was in addition to the thrice-weekly concerts for the refugees.

For those away from the bright lights and festivities at the Palace, Christmas 1914 was grim indeed. Since 11 September street lights, illuminated advertisements and the lights in shop windows had been reduced or extinguished. Public transport had windows fitted with blinds or curtains, vehicle lights were dimmed, illuminated clock dials were switched off as were lights on streets, bridges and river banks. The only permissible lights were those scouring the sky for Zeppelins. Public houses closed at 10.00 p.m. and cinemas closed on Sundays. Saturday night markets replaced their flares with dim oil lamps. Public clock chimes were silenced.

Deaths at the front were mounting, the weekly casualty lists in local and national newspapers lengthened, the numbers of wounded returning home escalating. August's optimism that the war would be over by Christmas now seemed foolish.

The cost of living had soared, with coal and other necessities in short supply. The price of food and fuel had risen sharply, with accusations of rich people hoarding both. The poor were worst hit as they could only afford to buy small quantities of coal at a time. Throwing away cinder waste became a punishable offence: newspapers carried tips on making briquettes from coal dust and cement.

The Poor Law rates set in November for the British-born wives and children of alien enemies were insufficient. The London weekly rate was 10s and 6d for the woman and 1s and 9d per

Right: *Christmas Day in the children's ward.*

Below: *The giant Christmas tree in the Great Hall with Alderman Sloper dressed as Father Christmas.*

child. Should a child leave school or die the money was reduced immediately. For families outside London the woman's rate was 9s and 3d.

Never one to miss an opportunity to swipe at the aliens, *John Bull* of 2 January 1915, printed the following letter: 'Sir, as you are so charitable to poor women and children, might one ask how you would suggest dealing with the British wives and children of German residents here? Would you only just hang them or have them starved to death?'

John Bull's reply: 'We should deal with them severely, if they were destitute, for having married Germhuns. Having locked up the husbands if suspicious, we should heap coals of fire on their heads by feeding their hungry. As we have said, this is a very charming country for Germhuns to marry in'.

The Times of 12 January offered a humane viewpoint on the suffering of these families. F.A. Robertson, Chairman of the Central Council of the United Aliens Relief Societies and Director of the Society of Friends of Foreigners in Distress, wrote:

> We have been able to deal directly with some 3,000, representing over 10,000 persons. We have spent some £12,000 since the war began: we only apply three tests in giving relief to those shown to be in need of it. Is the applicant an alien? Is he or she in distress? Is he or she of good character? The greater part of the work lies among women and children: a large proportion of the women are the English wives of aliens. The distress is very great and the claim of the peaceable alien of good character, thrown out of remunerative works and into dire distress by the outbreak of war, through no fault of his own, while living under the protection of this country, is a very strong one, and it is only such that we relieve.

The 'Brave Belgians' still attracted much attention in the local newspapers. The *Wood Green Herald* of 9 January 1915 reported that:

> ...in the last few days about 400 young Belgian Army Recruits from Canada have been accommodated at the Palace. They came with a view to proceeding to the Front. Some have already gone and others have gone to Salisbury to complete their training. They are stated to have resented the strict supervision under which they were placed at the Palace and when allowed out many became the worse for drink. Exciting scenes were witnessed at many of the public houses, the men becoming indignant when drink was refused. The assistance of the police had to be obtained to escort some of them back to the Palace. One young man was charged at Wood Green Police Court on Friday and discharged with a caution.

The following week's edition carried a story on Belgians who were running amok and assaulting the police. Four men were charged: Maurice Drouard (23) and Theodore Veredun (32) were charged with being drunk and disorderly, while Pierre Claeys (53) and Jean Francois Claeys (63) pleaded that the beer given to them by the English was too strong. Upon being discharged the men saluted.

By 29 March 1915 the Palace was empty of refugees. The Metropolitan Asylum Board's closing accounts showed that the number of Belgian refugees processed at the Palace totalled 32,000, a figure only slightly exceeded by Earls Court, 33,000 during the same period. As news spread of the vacating, the public's hope, that they would be allowed back

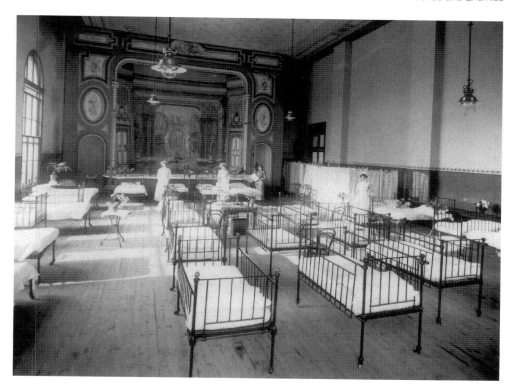

Above: *The Bijou Theatre used as a hospital.*

Right: *A new arrival – Albert Alexander – born at the Palace sometime between September 1914 and March 1915.*

The Navvies Battalion erecting barbed wire at the Palace, May 1915.

into the Palace, rose. Local newspapers pointed out that public access would be in the distant future as the Palace had been left in a sorry state with damaged furniture, carpets, radiators and hundreds of beds strewn around.

The Easter edition of the *Hornsey Journal* of 3 April ran the following article:

Alexandra Palace – Exit Belgians. What next?' Part of this read: 'The Belgians left with much regret and many tears. The Palace had been their haven of refuge for many months past before they have been transferred to the hospitable homes of England. Between three hundred and four hundred were in residence when the hour of parting came and they went afterwards to Olympia. There was a farewell gathering on the previous night where all the MAB staff, nurses and interpreters, and a few of the better class refugees had supper in one of the rooms of the Welcome Club. Members of the Alexandra Palace Orchestra, under Mr E.J. Parker, played selections and Miss Ethel Kemish and Mr E.W. Sloper sang. Mr Sloper, the Hon. Manager of the Palace, made a short speech expressing hope that everyone present would look back on their visit to the Alexandra Palace with pleasure. A deputation from the Belgians thanked Mr Sloper for what had been done for them at the Palace, and expressed gratitude for the kindness they had received in England, hoping that in happier times they would welcome their English friends to their own homes and return in some measure the kind treatment they had received in this hospitable land.

Long before the departure of the Belgians, the Palace Trustees had been in secret negotiations regarding the next influx. As the authorities departed in the wake of the last Belgians, Col John Ward and his Navvies Battalion moved in. They were soon at work erecting sentry boxes, strong fencing and barbed-wire entanglements to contain far more unwelcome guests, the Germans.

❧ SIX ❧

A GERMAN CIVILIAN PRISON

The Aliens Restrictions Act 1914 had decreed that all German and Austrian males between the ages of sixteen and forty-two were to be interned. As the authorities had no idea how many such men resided in the UK, the few places of imprisonment were soon overcrowded and could not cope. Olympia, the Isle of Man, prisons, workhouses, empty factories, race tracks and sports stadia, as well as passenger ships moored off the South Coast and Southend-on-Sea could not handle the huge influx. The situation was exacerbated by the arrival in Britain of large numbers of military prisoners of war. It was eventually agreed that only civilian aliens, who were perceived as a danger to the state, would be interned.

The torpedoing and sinking of the *Lusitania* by a German submarine off the coast of Ireland on 7 May 1915, with the loss of more than 1,500 lives, changed the situation dramatically. Following this, throughout London and the rest of the country violent anti-German riots erupted. After the suppression of the disturbances, on 13 May the Prime Minister Herbert Asquith declared in the House of Commons, amidst great applause, a new internment policy:

> All adult non-naturalised males between the ages of seventeen and fifty-five should, for their own safety and that of the community, be segregated or interned or, if over military age, repatriated.

Writing in *London during the Great War*, Michael McDonagh, who was in the House to witness Mr Asquith's speech, added that the Prime Minister refused to treat all naturalised aliens as spies and enemies. Most of them, Mr Asquith assumed, were loyal British subjects. Even the majority of the aliens who were not naturalised were, he believed, decent, honest people. At the conclusion of the Prime Minister's speech, McDonagh recorded that 'members of all parties were in so great a rage even against naturalised Germans that they were foaming at the mouth'.

The new order was effective almost immediately. Some aliens, fearing for their safety surrendered to their local police stations while others, fearful after the riots, fled and went into hiding.

Unsurprisingly, *John Bull* of 15 May bore opposing views to those of the Prime Minister. In an article entitled 'Now for the Vendetta! Vengeance is mine saith the Lord' Horatio Bottomley had a variety of suggestions of blood-curdling intensity of how to deal with 'the Hun'. These included unleashing on the battlefield Zulus and Basutos and other 'native and half civilised tribes' and let them run amok in the enemy's ranks. Mr Bottomley would give the Germans all the asphyxiating gas they wanted and would take no prisoners. He proposed hanging, drowning, and the extermination of every German-born man in Britain.

A few paragraphs later he suggests that German-born men should be placed on vessels such as mine sweepers or merchant ships in danger of German attack. Every German woman should be kept under lock and key, while both sexes should be forbidden to send or receive letters, at all times to wear badges proclaiming their nationality, while all children of such unions should not be allowed to attend any school, either public or private. He continued in similar vein the following week, concluding that '...there must be no person of German birth at large, free to give assistance and guidance to the enemy'.

Despite local opposition arrangements were well under way for the reception of the first contingents at the Palace. Work had started immediately the Belgians left. The *Wood Green Herald* of 7 May was able to inform its readers that in anticipation of the German prisoners the Palace had been cleared of the exhibits and amusements there during the presence of the Belgians, that a military guard (one of the City of London Regiments) was already in occupation of the building, and that barbed wire entanglements surrounding the outer part of the lower terraces was complete. This would ensure that the prisoners would be away from public view and, with the presence of armed sentries, would deter the prisoners from attempting escape.

John Bull of 1 May had already opined:

How long will it take to get out of the heads of the British government the idea that all the luxuries and comforts in this country we have to spare should be given to Germhun prisoners? Yesterday it was the luxuries of Donnington Hall; now it is the Elysium of the Alexandra Palace. Why should these atrocious enemies, without honour, without scruple and without pity be dumped down in this beautiful house and grounds – occupying one of the healthiest situations in the vicinity of London? Have not the officials who select places of internment for Germhun prisoners any imagination? Do they not realise that to intern them where every prospect pleases, and only man is vile, is an offence practically to the whole nation? If pleasances such as the Alexandra Palace and grounds are to be used for military necessities, let them be used for our own wounded and convalescent soldiers, brave men all who have fought their God's fight for us with their flags unstained and their humanity glorified before the world. There is, too, another side to the question. Within the grounds are innumerable nooks and crannies suitable for treacherous machinations and hiding places

NOTICE OF CHANGE OF NAME.

I, CHARLES BENNETT, heretofore called and known by the name of Carl Schneider, of 123, Wanstead Park Avenue, Manor Park, London, E., and who was born at North Leith, Scotland, and who has for many years been employed by the Atlantic Transport Line, DO HEREBY GIVE PUBLIC NOTICE that on the 15th day of this present month of March I did, for and on behalf of myself and my heirs and issue lawfully begotten, formally, wholly, absolutely and utterly renounce, relinquish and abandon the use of my said Christian and Surname of Carl Schneider, and then assumed and adopted and determined thenceforth in all records, deeds, documents and writings, in all actions, suits and proceedings, in all dealings, transactions, matters and things, and upon all occasions whatsoever, to use and subscribe the name of Charles Bennett instead of the said name of Carl Schneider. AND I GIVE FURTHER NOTICE that, by a deed poll, bearing date the said 15th day of March instant, duly executed and attested and enrolled in the Central Office of the Supreme Court of Judicature on the 16th day of the said month of March, I formally, wholly, absolutely and utterly renounced, relinquished and abandoned the said Christian and Surname of Carl Schneider, and declared that I had assumed, adopted, determined, and intended thenceforth, upon all occasions whatsoever, to use and subscribe myself by the name of Charles Bennett instead of Carl Schneider; and so as to be, at all time thereafter called, known, described, and distinguished by the name of Charles Bennett exclusively.
Dated this 17th day of March, 1915.

CHARLES BENNETT,

formerly

CARL SCHNEIDER.

Witness:
H. W. GUTHRIE,
Solicitor,
116, Chancery Lane.
London. E.C.   18-25

An advertisement showing a change of name, from the Stratford Express, *20 March 1915.*

for those seeking means of escape. It does not seem that any protest would convince the British authorities of the differences between treating Germhun prisoners with humanity and decency and treating them with luxurious and superfluous hospitality.

The *Wood Green Herald*'s readership was informed on 14 May that the first contingent of 500 were now imprisoned in the Palace, although 1,500 had been expected. To quote:

The arrivals include naval and military personnel, some still in uniform. They arrived by special train in the Palace sidings at around 7.00 p.m. in the evening, to be greeted by the military guard. Some are said to have come from German West Africa, others from Queensferry, Ireland, and more are expected at any time. At the present moment arrangements are not quite complete, but the work is proceeding rapidly, with eventual capacity for 4,500 prisoners. On Saturday morning they went out for an hour's exercise. As the barbed wire fencing was not completed they were under a strong military guard.

STADDON & SONS,
(Late THOMAS EVANS.)
Drapers and House Furnishers,
Ladies' and Children's-Outfitters.

TELEPHONE—EAST 3330.

359. 361, & 363, BARKING ROAD
3, 4, 5, & 6, BALAAM STREET,
PLAISTOW, LONDON, E.

To the Public of Plaistow, West & East Ham, Poplar, Canning Town, Custom House, & East London generally.

IN VIEW OF THE REGRETTABLE INCIDENTS WHICH HAVE OCCURRED RECENTLY, I WOULD LIKE TO MAKE MY POSITION PERFECTLY CLEAR, AND TO REMOVE ANY POSSIBLE DOUBT IN THE MIND OF ANY SINGLE PERSON AS TO MY NATIONALITY.

I SHOULD HAVE SUPPOSED THAT THERE WAS NO BRITISHER WHO COULD NOT SEE WITH HALF AN EYE THAT THE NAME

STADDON

WAS
ESSENTIALLY ENGLISH

"ENGLISH OF THE ENGLISH," INDEED. AS A MATTER OF FACT I WAS

BORN IN "GLORIOUS DEVON,"

WHERE MY PARENTS AND FOREFATHERS HAD FARMED FOR GENERATIONS, AND, WITH THE SINGLE EXCEPTION OF A DAY-TRIP TO CHERBOURG IN A CHANNEL STEAMER, WHICH I ONCE TOOK DURING A SUMMER VISIT TO THE SEASIDE, THERE IS NO RECORD OF ONE OF US EVER HAVING BEEN OUT OF THIS COUNTRY. I THEREFORE FOUND IT DIFFICULT TO UNDERSTAND HOW ANYONE COULD HONESTLY HAVE SUPPOSED THAT THERE WAS THE FAINTEST TRACE OF ANY BUT

PURE BRITISH BLOOD

IN MY VEINS. NO! IN COMMON WITH ALL OTHER INHABITANTS OF OUR DEAR OLD COUNTRY, I WAS DEEPLY HORRIFIED AND INCENSED WHEN I READ OF THE DIABOLICAL ACT OF THOSE ACCURSED MURDERERS IN SINKING THE "LUSITANIA" WITHOUT A MOMENT'S WARNING; BUT LITTLE DID I THINK THAT I SHOULD EVER BE SUSPECTED OF ANY CONNECTION WHATEVER WITH SUCH A NATION OF PIRATES AND POISONERS.

AT THE MOMENT WHEN UNWORTHY SUSPICION, NAY THREATS, WERE BEING DIRECTED AT ME, MY SONS AND NEPHEWS, WITH MY SANCTION AND HEARTY APPROVAL, WERE "DOING THEIR BIT" ON ACTIVE SERVICE ABROAD, AND HAVE BEEN ALMOST FROM THE COMMENCEMENT OF THE WAR.

MY BUSINESS—WHICH IS MINE AND MINE EXCLUSIVELY—HAS NOT A SINGLE HALFPENNY OF ANYONE ELSE'S MONEY IN IT; NEITHER HAS ANY OTHER PERSON, BRITISH OR FOREIGN, ANY INTEREST WHATEVER IN IT. SUCH AS IT IS, I AM RUNNING IT FOR AND BY MYSELF; AND WITH IT I SHALL HAVE TO SINK OR SWIM.

FROM THE VERY COMMENCEMENT OF MY PROPRIETORSHIP I WAS RESOLVED TO MAKE, WHAT WAS THEN A SOUND, HONEST BUSINESS, ADMIRABLY CONDUCTED BY MY MUCH RESPECTED PREDECESSOR—MR. THOMAS EVANS—OF STILL MORE SERVICE TO THE PUBLIC BY DEVOTING THE WHOLE OF MY ENERGIES AND WIDE EXPERIENCE TO GIVING THE PUBLIC THE

UTMOST POSSIBLE VALUE FOR THEIR MONEY.

MY EFFORTS FROM THE VERY FIRST WERE GENERALLY RECOGNISED, AND I AM PROUD AND PLEASED TO BE ABLE TO SAY THAT I HAVE MADE COUNTLESS FRIENDS AMONGST MY CUSTOMERS, WHOSE INTERESTS AND MY OWN I ALWAYS REGARD AS IDENTICAL.

Signed **T. C. STADDON.**

East London business proclaiming British nationality. East London Advertiser, *15 May 1915.*

In the same edition, Wood Green Notes added:

The strict military rule is now in force at the Palace, and the number of passes issued to secure admission to the grounds is limited to staff members. The news of the arrival of the first contingent of Germans on Friday soon spread and large crowds gathered on Saturday and Sunday to catch a glimpse of them. It was, however, utterly impossible. All that could be seen was a sentry pacing up and down with his fixed bayonet glittering in the sunshine. The barbed wire fences are far too near the Palace to permit of anyone being observed from the roadway, and hosts of sentries are there to see that the prisoners do not perform the humanly impossible task of wriggling out. Passes have to be shown nearly half a dozen times to get into the buildings, and the exchange of a word with a German entails the risk of being shot. Once more, however, the Palace terraces are outlined with bright high pressure gas lamps. Zeppelin attacks are not regarded as likely, and the lamps are useful to help the night sentries in their duties.

The *North Middlesex Chronicle* of 15 May reported that:

The German prisoners have arrived at the Palace and, as can be expected, formed the subject of public attention. The splendid weather which prevailed on Sunday afforded the opportunity of an expedition to the famous North London amusement centre. The crowds were able to view the German camp from afar and many caustic comments were made about the prisoners . . . from the Hornsey side of the Palace visitors looking across the racecourse grounds could see the Germans bathing in the sunshine and the armed sentries walking in the barbed wire enclosure. Despite the storm of protest at the beginning, the Germans are being guarded by volunteers.

Throughout the years crowds viewing their unwelcome German guests did so not in the spirit of friendly curiosity extended to their Belgian visitors. The mood was far more belligerent. Nine months of the war that had been expected to be over by Christmas had affected many of the population. The air raids, the sinking of the *Lusitania*, heavy losses at the front, the sound of the guns from France and the latest horror perpetrated by the Germans – mustard gas – soured many.

The Palace administration was also unhappy with the new arrivals. A letter sent to Alderman Sloper from the Defence of the Realm Losses Committee dated 17 May informed the Trustees that until 31 May the weekly sum of £250, as supplied for the Belgians, would continue to be paid. From 1 June this sum would be reduced to £225 a week. This included light, heating, water supplies, rates and taxes, with the cost borne from public funds. A lump sum of £140 was offered as compensation to the Palace catering staff who had lost their jobs when the War Office took over. Work would be found for the prisoners at a reasonable rate of pay in refurbishing the East Front of the Palace. It was also agreed that notice would be given to photographers Davey and Hackney to vacate their premises, and that a Mrs Wilson and Thompson's Gravity Switchback be requested to remove their buildings from Palace land.

Disaffection with the internees took many forms. A letter from 'Britain for Britons' appeared in the *Wood Green Herald* of 21 May. This referred to the recent riots as well as the spy peril posed by naturalised and non-interned wealthy Germans whom the Government refused to imprison. The letter concluded: 'The smouldering temper of the British bulldog has merely exposed its fangs in the recent rioting, but should it burst into flames there will be no aliens to intern; then heaven help the members of the Cabinet who have generated the conflagration by their pusillanimity'.

The same paper carried letters from naturalised Germans reiterating their loyalty to England and the Crown. Other letters made statements that the writers were not of German birth but of other European origin. All the writers expressed loyalty to their adopted country.

On 22 May Horatio Bottomley proclaimed that his editorial chair was a more powerful pulpit for the great force of public opinion than a seat in the House of Commons. The reason for this boast? In the previous week the King had expunged from the Roll of the Order of Garter the name and titles of the Kaiser and other German knights. In his usual fashion Bottomley claimed this was his suggestion as mooted in his article of 15 May. Whether this was truly the case is debatable.

The *Wood Green Herald* of 21 May reported that on Sunday the 16th Wood Green police had taken into custody four local unmarried registered aliens plus another four on Tuesday the 18th and sent them to the concentration camp at Frimley. The news item continued with the story that those removed on Sunday had met a volunteer corps on their route march. Some of the volunteers had shouted 'Goodbye Fritz, Goodbye Karl' and so on and the corps band played while proceeding along the route behind them.

While some prisoners were despatched to Frimley, the influx of internees to the Palace continued. In a long article in the edition of 29 May the *Hornsey Journal* reported that proposals to use the Palace as a convalescent home for soldiers had been turned down but to see '...[the Palace] inhabited by men of a race that has made the world cry with horror and disgust, the public would scarcely be human if they did not resent the malappropriation'. The article concluded: 'It [the Palace] offers a mark for the airship or aeroplane; but, ruthless as our enemies are, it is doubtful whether they would assail it with bombs if they know it is filled with their own countrymen. It is the only consoling thought in connection with the occupation of it by interned Germans'.

Anti-German feeling had been fanned again in the capital by the first Zeppelin air raid in London on 31 May and exacerbated by rumours that Germany was trying to recruit corps of spies from free Germans in the community.

Perhaps stung by the *Hornsey Journal*, Alderman Sloper issued a rebuttal in the *Wood Green Herald* of 4 June that '...the Trustees had tried their best to get the Palace used for convalescent soldiers but with no success'.

The *Tottenham and Edmonton Herald* of 9 June told its readers that there were now more than 3,000 Germans at the Palace; that two contingents had arrived the previous week via the Palace Gates railway station, being received there by an armed guard and marched up to the Palace. The paper reported that their arrival caused quite a stir; but there was nothing but perfect order, concluding that '...everything so far is peaceful in the "prison"'.

The *Daily Sketch* of 16 June carried the following apocryphal story entitled 'Delicacies Indeed!' The item read:

A woman came to a friend of mine in North London the other day and asked for money for a fund to be devoted to the purchase of delicacies for German prisoners interned in Alexandra Palace. She was quite serious; so was I when I asked if she was quite certain she was an Englishwoman. She was very hurt of course. So was I, and I drew her attention to the latest casualty list caused by the Air Hun – one man, two women, four children. Delicacies indeed!

Not missing a beat, *John Bull* of 19 June continued the theme with 'Hymns for Huns' indignantly reporting: 'What's this we hear about ladies of Muswell Hill singing to the Germhun prisoners interned at Alexandra Palace? If so, let them remember Belgium, and those women's vain cries for mercy that rent the shuddering air'.

The *Hornsey Journal* of the same date reported that at a meeting of the Harringay Business Association the internees provoked a variety of opinions. Mr C.H.S White raised the question of Germans at the Palace, stating that the great organ was used for recitals and that a grand piano was used at concerts. Mr George Brown added that: 'With the aid of field glasses he had seen football being played and German prisoners basking in the sunshine in that 'heaven-sent place', instead of wounded soldiers being accommodated there'.

In reply it was pointed out that organ recitals were given by Mr Cunningham to keep the organ in trim. If the prisoners cared to pay for grand pianos they could have them, just as our men could in Germany. The whole of the arrangements were in the hands of the War Office not the Trustees. Also, rumours that the statues in the Central Hall had been smashed were unfounded.

In the same edition, under the heading 'Pencils and Jottings' the writer, commenting on the meeting wrote that:

I fancy that the members were rather at sea in regard to the prisoners…the entertainments that are given are for the soldiers in their leisure hours and I should not be surprised to learn that the men engaged in cricket and football, whom Mr Brown saw through his spyglass, wear khaki during business hours. The wire entanglements do not enclose space enough for a cricket pitch or football ground. If they did it would not occasion much surprise. Did not one of our own Middlesex men write from Germany quite recently asking for footballs to kick around after a day's work? We are not going to be behind Germany in any form of 'Kultur', least of all the physical kind.

As the year progressed the number of internees at the Palace continued to grow. Often arriving by motor bus or van, the flow of new inmates continued to generate interest among the local population who regularly turned out to see them. The *Wood Green Herald* of 24 September reported the arrival of 350 internees thus:

A crowd had gathered at the Wood Green entrance to the Palace to watch the motorcade of buses which had begun at ten o'clock and continued until the late afternoon. There were fifty notices served and complied within each of the seven Metropolitan Police divisions. In the Wood Green sub division there were six internees – four at Wood Green and one each at Muswell Hill and New Southgate. The men presented themselves at Kentish

Town Police Station before being taken to Wood Green. There were few who 'waited to be fetched'. For the most part they attended the stations with their personal belongings in bags and parcels and chatted merrily among themselves until the omnibus was ready to take them to the camp.

The Times of 20 September had also reported an influx. Their article read: 'The London police arrested on Saturday and took for internment at Alexandra Palace 350 enemy aliens – fifty each from the Marylebone, Paddington, Whitechapel, Hackney, Islington, Hampstead and Highgate districts. The prisoners are all men of military age – Germans from seventeen to fifty-five and Austrians from seventeen to fifty-one, mainly hairdressers, waiters and hotel employees, but two stockbrokers are among the number'.

On 27 September *The Times* reported the arrival of a further party believed to be in the region of 800 were to be interned – some at the Palace while others would go to the camp at Stratford in East London. The article stated:

> This action follows notices issued on the previous Friday by the police, acting under instructions from the Home Office, warning all aliens who had failed to secure exemptions to hold themselves ready for internment. During Saturday many aliens visited the Home Office in the hope of obtaining special treatment but were informed that the decision was final. At a meeting of the Anti-German Union at Peckham Rye yesterday, it was stated by one of the speakers that the Pastor of the German church at Forest Hill, who had closed the doors rather than not carry out services in German, had been interned.

The Times of the following day, repeating much of what had been written previously, concluded: 'The men included a considerable number of German hairdressers. There were a few prisoners who had been holding responsible positions. One batch arrived at the Palace in a furniture van. Others came in brakes and two or three in taxis'.

The *Wood Green Herald* continued to take a lively interest in the newcomers, and in its edition of 1 October wrote: 'They brought with them all sorts and sizes of bundles of clothing, bags and baskets and were a very mixed lot, from top hats and frock coats down to rags and tatters. To make room for the newcomers there was a clearance of several hundred Germans from the Palace last week, a large contingent being sent to the Isle of Man. The number at the Palace remains at about 4,000.'

The paper also reported that the Trustees had purchased plant and tools from the Central (Unemployed) Body so that internees at the Palace could be set to work.

As the numbers increased, the Society of Friends delegated W.R. Hughes to make regular visits to the Palace and form a Committee of internees. All the men would be encouraged to use any skills they had to make articles for sale, both in this country and overseas. These would be promoted by the Society of Friends. The Society's input to the Palace, as well as other camps, would include work of a pastoral nature, plus liaison between the prisoners and outside authorities.

The war, which many had predicted would be over by Christmas in 1914, trudged wearily into 1916. This would be a year of austerity for everyone and tragedy for some, whether civilian, soldier or those 'inside the wire'.

❧ SEVEN ❧

INTERNED

In no previous war had European enemy civilians been interned. The Germans in England, the foreigners of enemy nations in all countries, must not be allowed to join the belligerent forces of their own countries of origin and they must not be allowed to endanger the safety of the countries they happened to be in when war broke out. They were therefore rounded up and locked away in camps because that was the easiest way of dealing with the problem.

Time Stood Still, Paul Cohen-Portheim, 1932

During the early months of its new function, Alexandra Palace was used as a clearing house with parties of men arriving and departing, some being dispersed to the Isle of Man camps at Douglas and Knockaloe. Also part of this transience were Germans and Austrians transferred from the prison ships moored off Southend-on-Sea and along the South Coast, aliens who had been arrested in the 'sweeps' and held in the tented camp at Frimley in Surrey while others had been living in tents, horse boxes and stables at Newbury racecourse, where six to eight men bedded on straw, with neither heat or light, being locked up at sunset until the next morning. Many complaints were received by the camp authorities about the potential danger to health because of the rigorous conditions. Fearful of rioting among the prisoners, the camps were eventually condemned and closed.

The prison ships – former passenger vessels the *Royal Edward* (afterwards sunk in the Mediterranean while on transport work) and the *Saxonia* were moored in the Thames off Southend. On board the *Royal Edward* there were 1,400 prisoners, with the interned men divided into three classes, each class having as its quarters that part of the vessel designed for the use of the first, second or third class of ordinary passengers. The first-class prisoners paid for part of their own food, and were at liberty to engage servants from the third class. The second and third class received free of charge the standard rations and for those in third class free clothing was issued when needed. On the *Saxonia* there were about 1,200 prisoners, all deemed to be of the third class. At Portsmouth there were some 2,000 prisoners interned on the *Ascania* and *Manitoba*. These again were divided into three classes. On the *Tunisian*, moored off the Isle of Wight, there were many complaints about medical treatment and food, and some prisoners resorted to throwing letters in bottles over the side to complain about their grievances.

The overcrowded insanitary conditions on the boats were highly unsatisfactory and eventually the boats were abandoned, with prisoners being moved to either Alexandra Palace or the Isle of Man. It is estimated that approximately 17,000 men passed through Alexandra Palace in transit to other destinations. Despite this turmoil, a resident population of about 3,000 men settled there.

German Richard Notschke was first interned at the Stratford jute factory before being transferred to Alexandra Palace in 1917. Married to an English woman, the father of three daughters and two sons (one of whom would serve with the British Army) he had been employed in the City by the same firm for over twenty years. This ended when he was dismissed on 18 December 1914. His memoirs describe his difficult life after the outbreak of war until his arrest on 16 July 1915. Despite many attempts to find work elsewhere, sometimes securing jobs before being forced to leave because of intimidation to his sympathetic employers, he eventually found employment by masquerading as a Russian. This did not last. Richard Notschke wrote:

> I received notice from the Home Office to be prepared for internment at an early date, in the meantime the Germans had sunk with theyr submarine the great Ship the *Lusitania*. The action eraged the people of England to such a pitch as the World had never known before, and on the evening of the 12th of May the mob in London run mad and had theyr revenge on all the German bussiness places. It started as if all arranged by signall all in one night and over a thousand German shops and some private houses were shmashed to pieces, the furniture thrown in the street and smashed, and in many instances burned. The authorities seemed powerless or did not seem to want to interfere. This rioting took place for severall nights; very few people were charged. It seemed strange as if the authorities seemed to approve of it; up to midnight I heard the breaking of glass and shmashing of furniture and what they did not break they looted. At eleven o'clock at night I received notice that now the private houses would be attacked. I fastened my door but the mob did not come so far but remained in the main street. Nobody can imagine the position in which we Germans found ourselves.

It has long been believed that the riots were not spontaneous but were orchestrated by trouble makers the length and breadth of Britain. Sylvia Pankhurst maintained that hunger was the cause, which may well have played its part, but there is much evidence that one of the primary motives was revenge.

Newspapers from the Northcliffe stable, such as the *Daily Mail*, the *Evening News* and tub-thumping, rabble-rousing *John Bull*, whipped up a frenzy of German hatred. A rhyme of the day went:

Above: *The tented camp for interned civilians at Frimley, Surrey.*

Right: *Internment – internees being taken to the prison ships at Southend.*

MAY 29TH, 1915. JOHN BULL. 21

The Anti-German Pledge

If you cannot fight in the Field, will you take the Pledge—THE ANTI-GERMAN PLEDGE—and help us to smash the Germans commercially?

THE OBJECTS OF THE LEAGUE.

(1) To enrol a Million Members who will take the Anti-German Pledge.

(2) To amend the law relating to Alien Immigration, and the Naturalisation of Germans as British subjects.

(3) To legislate for a protective, and if necessary a prohibitive tariff on all German and Austrian-made goods.

(4) To investigate German Patents, Processes, and Monopolies, with a view to imparting knowledge and information to British traders, manufacturers, and others who desire to work the same.

(5) To render financial and other assistance, with or without interest, to British Manufacturers who will undertake the production of goods hitherto made in Germany and Austria.

(6) To assist in returning to Parliament, any Candidates, irrespective of party, who will pledge themselves to support the objects of the League, and generally to arrange a series of Lectures in all the great Towns and cities throughout the Country, for the purpose of obtaining public support and approval.

THE PLEDGE.

I hereby sincerely and conscientiously promise (a) Not to purchase, use, or consume German, or Austrian goods of any kind whatever. (b) Not to employ a German for either domestic, or commercial purposes. (c) Not to place Contracts with any German-owned, or controlled Company, Trust, or Corporation, or to send goods by, or travel in, German Ships. (d) To boycott, and assist in the boycotting of, any trader who persists in stocking German, or Austrian goods, while British goods of equal quality and price are available. (e) To hold no intercourse socially, or commercially with Germans, and to ostracise from all respectable society every British-born woman who marries a German subject.

"JOHN BULL" COUPON FOR MEMBERSHIP.

To the Secretary,
THE ANTI-GERMAN LEAGUE,
25, Victoria Street, Westminster, S.W.

Dear Sir,—

I am willing to sign the Anti-German Pledge, and shall be glad if you will send me Application Form for Membership, Certificate, and Official Badge. I enclose 1s. for the first year's subscription, together with the sum of £.......... being a voluntary donation to your Funds.

Name (in full) ....

Address ....

NOTE.—Any further payment beyond the yearly subscription of 1s. is quite optional and voluntary, but will be gratefully accepted. Cheques and Postal Orders should be made payable to the Anti-German League, and crossed "London County & Westminster Bank."

It is the duty of every Englishman and every Englishwoman in the Country to sign this Pledge.

Will you do your duty?

To make it a popular movement within the reach of all, the purely nominal subscription for membership has been fixed at 1s. per annum, the object being universal interest, rather than a smaller number of rich subscribers; but we believe that there are many people in sympathy with the objects of the League who will subscribe su**b**stantially far beyond the actual membership fee, in which case our income will be materially augmented, and our scope of operations considerably enlarged.

The New Battle Cry: "Everything German Taboo."

A Million Members Wanted! ENROL AT ONCE!

Left: *Anti-German propaganda as seen in* John Bull, *29 May 1915.*

Below: *Anti-German propaganda – kicking out the Kaiser.* John Bull, *22 May 1915.*

THE ORDER OF THE GARTER—

—AND THE ORDER OF THE BOOT!

Beware the Jingo-Wock, my son
The lips that sneer, the lies that catch,
Beware the John-Bull bird and shun
The frumious Northcliffe batch!

During the riots a German man in East London was observed fleeing in terror from a court adjacent to Kingsland Road. He was pursued by a crowd of angry women, who abused and pelted him. With his clothing torn to tatters and his face streaming with blood, the man dashed to a stationary tramcar, and despite the frenzied efforts of the women to pull him off, he clambered to the upper deck. Followed upstairs by the infuriated women they continued their attack as the tramcar moved away. The conductor advised the man to leave the car at Shoreditch, which he did, darting away down a side street, an absolute wreck. Following the first Zeppelin air raid of 31 May 1915 on East London, Sylvia Pankhurst described seeing a man in flour-covered clothing being kicked and beaten: "'Orl right, Gov'ner; orl right" he articulated between the blows, in Cockney tones, fully typic as those of his assailants'.

Richard Notschke wrote:

On Wednesday the 21st of July I received notice from the Police that I will be interned on Friday the 23rd and that I have to represent myself at 9.00 a.m. at the East Ham police station for internment. So my time of freedom was expired. I packed my belongings, and on the Friday morning I wished my family goodbye and represented myself at 9.00 a.m. at the Police Station as ordered. Here I found one man already and another one soon came so we were three, and after a short preliminary by the Police Official we were taken by three detectives: each had one of us in charge, by tramway to Stratford Camp. It was in Carpenter's Road, Stratford, Ritchies works, an old disused jute factory.

As we arrived here, there were also many others from all over London who came at the same time in pantechnicons and cabs. We were all bundled in to a small courtyard (or fore-yard). Here we were handed over by our gardiens to the Military Authoritys. For the first time we tasted here the rule of English Military kindness. We were all arranged in rows of two by some soldiers and pushed and shuffed about, so that our luggage could be searched, and now we had to pack out all our belongings on to the ground. It was raining hard at the time and had been raining all morning, but it was of no use protesting, here everything in the shape of scissors, pocket knives, rasors, writing paper, stamps, all sorts of small tools, and also money of over £1 was taken away, every protest against such unwarranted action brought only a shower of abuse from our Military guardians.

A burly sergeant Major made it his special duty to push the men's hats – caps of to see if anything was hidden away, he shouted in a loud voice, stand still, say yes sir when you are spoken to, and punched with his fist the men in the back and in the neck so their hats fell to the ground. The Officer in charge, to his everlasting disgrace may it be said took no notice, and let them have a free hand. All the articles wich they took away we never saw no more nor received any compensation for them. At last the great iron doors opened and we were driven like cattle and shut in. Here inside represented a picture which I will try to describe as near I can. About 400 men allready inside this great old factory all standing arround and waiting for new arrivals. Many had allready been in there for nearly a year, and many knew each other

Anti-German riots: crowds looting a German shop (above) and a German house in Poplar (below).

from outside London life, or had not seen each other for years, here they all meet again. In one corner was a kind of Registry Office, fitted up and carried on by our own Countrymen to help the Military Authorities. Each of us newcomers had to fill up a form. Prisoner of War where and when born, when captured and then received a number. I had the lucky one 3464. After all this we were devided in to twenty-four Man as a Mess, and then were shown the strawsacks as theyr future beds, which were placed on little woodden structures about six inches from the ground and about nine inches appart so that one could hardly get in between. Each man then received two blankets and that was all so far. The stawsacks were in a most filthy condition and also the blankets, as allready a good many who had been through this camp had slept in them before. The roof of this old factory was so bad, as soon as it rained it came through like a siff, but there was no chance of escaping it, but there was no room and I had to sitt many a night with a jam pot to catch the rain, or I would have drowned in bed. The floor was of stone or cement, in places full of holes of old machine parts, the old Transmission and wheels were hanging still in they'r places, all surrounded with barbed wire. The drainage was very old and too small for such a large roof, and at times of heavy rains or thunderstorms it used to come up the drains and swamp the place so that many of the strawsacks were floating about.

Notschke continues:

And now, referring back to the days of my first internment, after we had been lodged in this veritable hell, our families had no idea of what had become of us, and where we had been sent to. We were not allowed to write for a week, than we all made a petition to the Commandant to allow us to inform our famillies of our whereabouts. He was so kind and allowed each of us to write a postcard only after that knew our wives what had become of us. After we had been in there for a month we were allowed to receive a visit from our wives. I had exactly eight minutes. We had to sit on a table opposite to each other guarded by soldiers and in the presence of an officer and the camp interpreter. The second month we had half an hour, and later on it was actually one hour per month.

Notschke recounts some of the petty cruelties inflicted on the prisoners, such as the refusal by the authorities to allow men out to visit their dying wives and children, unless by order of the Doctor assigned to the Camp and permission from the Home Office. This all took so long that frequently the person had died and only then was the man allowed to attend the funeral in charge of a soldier guard. He cites several instance of telegrams notifying a prisoner of impending death that were only handed to the man after the funeral. He adds that five men went mad and several died.

Another description of the Stratford Camp is related in the memoirs *Time Stood Still* by Paul Cohen-Portheim, a German theatrical costume designer, interned while travelling in London from his home on the Continent. Shortly after the sinking of the *Lusitania* he was arrested and taken in a taxi to Stratford, with a policeman and three elderly men who worked in the City. He writes:

The taxi stopped in a narrow dirty lane. Gates again, another courtyard, a factory. No more police; soldiers and officers instead. The luggage was sorted out, soldiers started examining it. An officer stood by, watching the scene indifferently. I entered the building, as I had seen others do before me. I was faced by a very large glass roofed hall, with a good deal of its glass broken. The floor was tightly packed with beds, or rather palliasses lying on a kind of bedstead; there were crowds of men standing about, sitting or lying fully dressed on these couches and numbered, as I learned later, about 1,000. We got some sort of soup, with bits of meat swimming about in it, served in metal pots. I had been given a couch, why not unpack. But where did one's things go? I asked a bundle of rags lying on the next couch – much to his amusement. There's nowhere he grinned, you just took what you needed; personally he had long given up changing for the night, or the day either. I felt so helpless, was one to sit or lie on a sack and have verminous neighbours who would steal one's things lying next to one?

The broken glass roof had been done by a Zeppelin raid. [Richard Notschke had complained of this, when rain came in through the roof, saturating bedding and clothing, and allowing bird to nest, whose droppings frequently fell on the prisoners and into their food]. The lights went out at ten, only a few very bright lamps remained on; the air was thick, with people already beginning to snore – sleep seemed impossible. A man walked by quickly, holding together his scanty garments with one hand, the other raised to the sky. A few more followed. That was what you had to do if you wished to visit the lavatory. I thought of the men who had been in the taxi with me, middle-aged stockbrokers or something of intense respectability, waving their arms in the air if they wished to…'

The next day Cohen-Portheim was transferred to the Isle of Man and thence to Wakefield.

An article in the *British Medical Journal* of 4 November 1916, written by a Lt Col Ronaldson Clark, MB, MRCP, a medical referee at the Home Office, was an angry rebuttal of an earlier article written by a Dr zum Busch which appeared on 27 July in *Deutsche Medeizinische Wochenschrift*. This article affirmed many of Richard Notschke's experiences. Dr zum Busche described the rain pouring through the broken glass roof and flooding the stone floors. Lt Col Ronaldson Clark's choleric response was: 'As a matter of personal observation I can vouch that there is not a stone flag anywhere in the floor of the sleeping room. It is of concrete and wood in alternate strips each about six feet broad, so that Dr zum Busche's account of the great puddles of water which are collected between the stone flags must be entirely imaginative'. The Lt Col also passed comment on Dr zum Busche's description of the food, saying:

> The cooking is done by some of the interned civilians who have been chefs or cooks in first class hotels or on board passenger ships, and the meals that I have seen on the many surprise visits I have made to the Stratford camp which have all been sufficient, well cooked and appetizingly served. I have inspected both the meat and fish before they were cooked both at Stratford and other camps, and can certify they are both of excellent quality and quite as good, if not better, than the ration meat which is served to our troops in the field. Zum Busch's statements about "poor quality, tasteless white bread, small portions of frozen meat and insufficient vegetables" are nothing more than mischievous lies.

Had the Lt Colonel asked Richard Notschke and the other prisoners he would have discovered the good doctor told nothing but the truth.

❧ EIGHT ❧

INSIDE THE WIRE

Early arrivals at the Palace included the Society of Friends' Emergency Relief Committee, supervised by W.R. Hughes, and M. Kastner, Chairman of the Doctor Märkel Committee.

Among early internees was Rudolf Rocker, a well-known socialist author who remained there until his repatriation to Germany in March 1918. He became the leader of 'B' Battalion, one of three designated A, B and C, each of which contained 1,000 men. Each battalion had its own compound, kitchen, lavatories and bathing facilities. Battalions were divided into ten companies, each company containing twenty-five men. Every man was provided with a bed, straw mattress, pillow and blankets. A small cake of soap was supplied free weekly, for personal washing and laundry. Because of the closeness between each bed, there was little privacy or space to store belongings. The space was so limited that constant bodily contact was unavoidable. When men laid at night on the straw sacks and stretched both arms out, they could not do so without touching their immediate neighbours. Rocker said: 'Never is he for even a single instant alone: his most intimate and discreet physical needs can only be satisfied in the company of others'.

W.R. Hughes of the Society of Friends visited Alexandra Palace in late February 1916. Part of his report stated:

> I spent time in the hospital talking with individual prisoners. It was interesting to hear from a man whose comrades at Knockaloe had paid his fare to London to visit his dying wife, and who is now at the Palace, a comparison of the two camps. He says that the conditions at Knockaloe are rather rougher, but he would rather be there because the twenty men in a hut section could live together like a large family, whereas at the Palace several hundred men lived and slept together and could not get away from each other.

At first, men were not allowed to have any small tables, stools or even boxes for keeping foodstuff, etc. near their beds. The commandant ensured his rule was never contravened. Although not prompted by malice, he had no knowledge of the real necessities of the prisoners. However, the severest military restrictions were unable to uphold this decision. From old boxes the prisoners made small and primitive tables, chairs and cupboards which infringed the regulations but could not be suppressed, so at last the new conditions were accepted.

Initially there was a time when the men of the various battalions were forbidden to communicate with each other. After the morning head count they were sent down to their respective barbed-wire enclosures, and forced to remain there until midday. Walking upon the terraces was strictly forbidden. Rocker said: '…and so it happened that when a prisoner was overcome by a natural desire, he would have to ask one of the guards for permission to satisfy his necessity. "Find five others" was the usual reply and, having been found, the six delinquents were marched up, between fixed bayonets, to the place of relief'.

Part of a report on Christmas preparations written by W.R. Hughes of 17 December 1915 described these as:

> …going forward vigorously. Fifteen men are working until midnight packing parcels. The [Prisoners'] Committee's Christmas greetings will be included in these. Others were preparing paper decorations and I saw Christmas trees arriving. A special Christmas card, with a picture of the Palace, is being sold to the men. Altogether there is a fund of £300 available for Christmas. Upon a request coming from Mrs Garrett-Smith, one or two of the men are constructing a large model hospital ship for use at the Christmas celebrations in the children's ward of St Thomas's Hospital.

A 'neutral' visited the Palace shortly before Christmas 1915. His article in *The Times* of 21 December 1915, describes entering the Palace grounds, passing through 'thick barbed wire entanglements running across the well kept lawns' and entering rooms where the internees were enjoying visits from their families.

He continued:

> In the kitchens of Alexandra Palace I saw not only row upon row of excellent bread, both white and brown made to suit the taste of the prisoner, but pan upon pan of jam filled doughnuts, apple tarts and teacakes with raisins as well as other delicacies. The meat is of good quality and half a pound per day is allowed each man, who also receives one and a half pounds of bread daily. It must be recalled that in German camps only half a pound of bread is allowed daily to each man and that it is a black, indigestible mixture, while meat is the exception rather than the rule.

He then describes the battalions:

> The cots are three wooden boards – raised four inches from the floor – on which is placed a straw mattress. Each man has two woollen blankets and a pillow, there are about three feet between each cot. The halls are partitioned off in groups of about fifty cots, and a man has

Internees in their compound – eastern front of Palace.

a small cabinet for his personal effects and hooks for his clothing. The halls are heated by coal stoves and gas hot water heaters. It is difficult to convince myself this is a war prison.

The pictures of British prisoners in Germany rise before me. Herded in box stalls, in stable lofts and temporary huts, the men there are undergoing great physical hardships. The surroundings are bleak and ugly. Alexandra Palace is truly a palatial prison of war.

The Times reporter Michael McDonagh visited the Palace a week later, on 28 December. He wrote:

Today I visited Alexandra Palace, those extensive buildings and grounds, where close on a thousand civilian prisoners of war, males of military age, are interned. They are German subjects who lived and carried on their avocations in London. Male Germans who were scattered about the provinces are interned in the Isle of Man. Some are still allowed to be at large, for special reasons. Most of those at Alexandra Palace are waiters, barbers, cooks, bakers and tailors. There are also several who held responsible positions as hotel managers and commercial agents.

They are provided by the military authorities, in whose charge they are, with four meals a day – including one and a half pounds of bread, half a pound of meat (on Fridays fish is served instead of meat), twelve ounces of vegetables, butter, tea and coffee. Their games are tennis in the grounds and chess indoors. There are barbers' shops. The morning charges for hair cutting is four-pence and for shaving twopence. In the afternoons these charges are reduced by half. Waiting and cleaning up are done in turns by the poorer class of prisoners, for which they are paid a few shillings a week. The better off pay two shillings and sixpence a week for such attendance, and have separate cubicles at an extra charge of one shilling a night. Circles have been formed for the learning of languages and general study. Commercial men are allowed to conduct their businesses. Wives and children may visit the Palace once a week. British born wives are paid sustenance allowances by the state. On the whole the prisoners seem comfortable and contented, as well they may.

The *Wood Green Herald* of 31 December 1915 told of the 'German Prisoners' Christmas Dinner' despite admitting that 'no official information was available on how German prisoners in London spent Christmas' but every opportunity was given to them to enjoy Christmas in their own way: 'It was unofficially stated that at Alexandra Palace and elsewhere, the prisoners dined off roast pork, their favourite dish, with a plentiful supply of vegetables'.

Not to be outdone, the *Daily Mail* of 13 January 1916 reported a visit to Alexandra Palace by an Ella Hepworth Dixon. Describing the views from the Palace, she writes: 'So, Hans and Fritz, the waiter and the barber, and the Herr Ferdinand Tuchmann, late of the London Stock Exchange – who paces the terrace, clad in clothes from Savile Row and smoking a fat cigar – will suffer from no atrophy produced by limited horizons'. She described the Great Hall, home of 'B' Battalion:

At the first blush you might think you were at some monster fête where many had come to camp, for the Great Hall is gay with innumerable festoons of coloured paper, made by the prisoners to celebrate Christmas and New Year. You look down on rows and rows of beds and hope, probably in vain, that the English civilians at Rühleben have half such chances of keeping warm, aired and comfortable. It is after luncheon and one or two of the aliens are indulging in the Teutonic habit of the Schläfchen, or short afternoon sleep. As, indeed, being free to do as they please, they have every right to do so.

Upon visiting the kitchens she comments in similar vein to Michael McDonagh, adding: 'A liberally supplied canteen is at their disposal to buy extras, which includes most things excluding alcohol in any form'. She describes card playing, reading and studying languages, with Spanish allegedly a favourite, for: 'Even the most fatuous Boche is beginning to realise that neither England nor her Dominions will extend open arms to him after the war, and that Brazil, Patagonia or Peru will be the chief area of his activities'.

Richard Notschke remained at the Stratford Camp, enduring the conditions he described until his request for a transfer to Alexandra Palace was granted in February 1917. He writes: 'When I first got on my way to the Palace everything seemed so strange, I was like a bird out of a cage. The people all looked at me as I was in charge of a soldier, but no one spoke'.

Notschke arrived at Alexandra Palace on 20 February and wrote: 'Here I was wellcomed by hundreds who used to be in Stratford from 1915–16 and had been in the Isle of Man, but had been sent back to London on account of theyr English wives as after two years internment the English government thought it more human that at least some men with English wives and children should come back to London so that theyr families could visit them'.

Programme for the first Christmas concert at the Palace, 3 December 1915.

A Christmas card sent by an internee.

He described the Palace:

> It seems like a new life as the place is beautifully situated on a hill surrounded by nice grounds and lovely trees. I had never seen a tree nor a green field all the time I was in Stratford. Here in this large building were 3,000 Germans interned, mostly all men with English wives, devided in three battalions – A, B and C. After I was registered at the Main Office I was handed over to 'B' Battalion, right in the centre of the main building. The place made a most peculiar impression, the Hall was about ninety feet high, on the further end a large organ, right round the whole hall the figures of all the Kings of England, and in the middle about a thousand strawsacks all more or less surrounded by blankets, canvas or other fancy material put up on four sticks like huts. It seemed like an Oriental Bazar or like a kind of Jerusalem. The tables were all arranged allong one side and looked very dirty. I received the number 12460 and was placed with the 12 Company, on table 26 but there was one great evil, utensils for cleanliness seemed very scarce, the very buckets in wich the soup was served were also used for washing up, and in most instances washing the floor. The atmosphere was at times unbearable, the wash and bath arrangement very bad. It was very difficult to get warm water, and to dry the washing but we had to do somehow. In foggy days sometimes the doors were not opened for four days the stench became unbearable.

The separation from wives and families brought many troubles, aggravated by the fact that prisoners could only write a very limited number of brief letters which, with the strict censorship, meant many letters took eight to ten days to arrive at their destinations. For men interned in the London camps, visits by wives and families were permitted once a month, later weekly, but those interned on the Isle of Man spent many years without an opportunity of meeting their families. Rocker wrote:

> To the superficial disinterested visitor, or to a press reporter, these things (the emotional stress of internment) may not be so apparent. Alexandra Palace is situated on a hill, commanding a good outlook over a large part of London; and during a fine day this view is by no means without its attractions. [On visiting days] both visitors and prisoners are attired in holiday dress, children enliven the scene and maybe the prisoner of war orchestra is playing during the visit. Such a visitor will conclude that this is only one of the many pleasures of intern-ment, of which he had read much in the newspapers, and very possibly will express the idea that internment is not such a bad thing. He will be blind to the silent tragedies being enacted around him.

Michael McDonagh, writing in *London during the Great War* describes this experience while sitting on high ground at Royal Wimbledon Golf Course: 'Thuds from the battle in France shook the earth. What was it? It was the terrible cannonade of the great battle in France, which was shaking the earth literally and indeed the whole world metaphorically. Not for long was I able to stand the sinister sensation! It affected my nerves. I got up and hastened away'.

For many of the internees at Alexandra Palace unable, like Michael McDonagh, to hasten away and already suffering mental stress, these occurrences added an extra poignancy to

'B' Battalion – living and sleeping accommodation in the Great Hall.

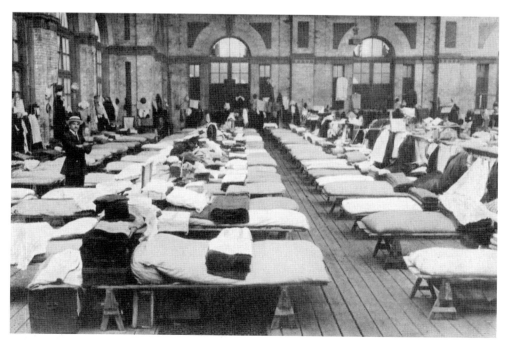

Smaller accommodation for 'A' Battalion but just as cramped.

their captivity: many had sons in the British forces and perhaps brothers and other relatives serving in the German army.

Rudolf Rocker also describes many internees who, feeling themselves on the verge of nervous collapse, deliberately committed minor violations of the camp rules in order to be locked away in solitary confinement for a few days, while others wrote to the Camp Commandant directly with the same request.

W.R. Hughes states: 'In some men the strain of camp life was very apparent. There is a recognised word applied to a man who starts muttering to himself or shows signs of melancholy. It is called the 'Camp Vogel'.

Rocker describes many of the internees: 'Even in fine weather one finds them lying on their beds, gazing languidly into space or sleeping away the brightest hours of the day in the fitful unhealthy sleep of the mentally depressed'.

Dr A.L. Vischer, who worked officially in both British and German camps, published a book on the 'Camp Vogel' in 1919, entitled *Barbed Wire Disease*. He described the first signs of problems as peculiarities of behaviour or temper. Interests were lost, solitude sought, muttering to oneself, becoming suspicious of comrades, fearing persecution or disease, memory loss and losing powers of attention. In bad cases the man would be subject to outbursts of hysteria and raving.

For those who succumbed to 'Camp Vogel', many were removed to the London County Asylum at Colney Hatch, New Southgate. Part of a report dated 31 July 1917 states that at the time of the visit from the Swiss Legation there were about 3,000 patients, of whom forty-four were civilian prisoners of war. The report continues: 'The German patients are not in a special ward, but according to their diseases, have been placed among the British patients and receive exactly the same nutrition and treatment. The institution ranks among the best lunatic asylums we have seen here, or in other countries. The German patients there deserve pity because they are ill, not because they are prisoners'.

One of the signatories was Dr A.L. Vischer, special attaché, who would later describe these experiences in *Barbed Wire Disease*.

Part of a report on a visit to Alexandra Palace on 14 March 1916 by the Swiss Legation referred to the sense of despair experienced by the internees, many with British-born wives and children, reinforcing the men's inability to do anything for their families, knowing their wives have to manage on the few shillings a week they received from the Board of Guardians. One man, whose wife had died, was informed that his children had been taken to the workhouse, while another discovered that his family had been evicted from their home for non-payment of rent, his wife choosing to buy food with the money instead. There were many such stories.

Rudolf Rocker stated that he had known men who would rather have remained on the Isle of Man, merely to be spared the distress of the knowledge in which their families were placed. He continued: 'And these were by no means unfeeling or callous men; it was simply the acute sense of their own helplessness and inability to alleviate the lot of their dearest ones which caused such expressions… His tenderness being thus increased, he will feel the wants and humiliations of his family, often more keenly than his own. Thus, while on the one hand he is rendered impotent, on the other he feels his obligations more keenly – his sufferings so being multiplied'.

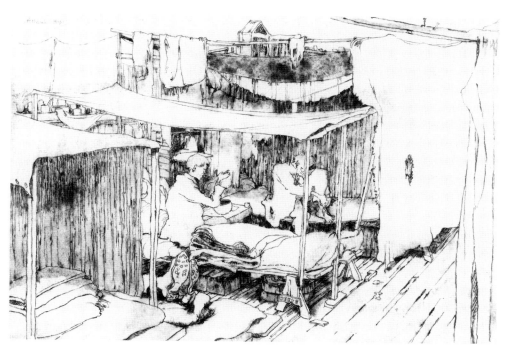

Prisoners in their home-made 'dormitory huts', as depicted by interned artist Rudolf Sauter.

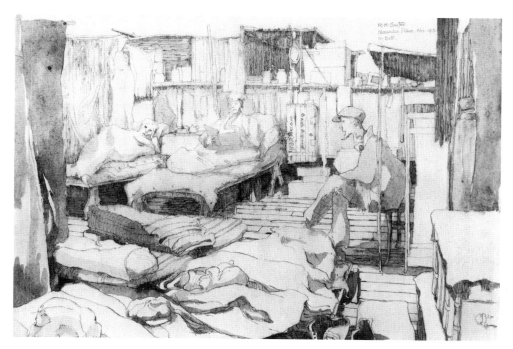

Sleeping prisoners in their 'dormitory huts', as depicted by interned artist Rudolf Sauter.

Left: *Painting of unknown internee's child, 1916.*

Opposite: *Letter from internee to wife, 1917.*

'In September 1916', related Rudolf Rocker, 'a large number of married men were transferred to Alexandra Palace from Knockaloe on the Isle of Man. What a poor appearance they presented, both as regards costume and habits, and how, gradually, the effect of seeing their families once a week changed them in a very marked manner. Their feelings on seeing their children again after so many months have been vividly and pathetically portrayed to me by some of them'.

While family visits were eagerly awaited, once they were over physical exhaustion and depression would set in as the men reflected upon the news from outside. A smallpox outbreak in March 1918, temporarily stopped visits from East London.

For some, anxieties surfaced upon their wives' fidelity and, aware of the campaign to offer British women divorces, looked for signs of disinterest, worried about missed visits and feared for their children. Rudolf Rocker adds: 'Their wives are held up to contempt, and if they are British-born are openly asked to prove their loyalty by forsaking their husbands'. With all these factors in mind and where a marriage had been less than successful, frequently the man turned upon his wife, venting his rage and frustration upon her and their children. For other men, their marriages were beyond repair, for a variety of reasons.

The lack of good quality food played its part in the camp's air of malaise. Despite assertions in the daily papers – especially those from the Northcliffe stable – of the well-fed 'Hun', the quality and quantity of the food deteriorated.

Richard Notschke, recently arrived at Alexandra Palace, at first found no cause for complaint but by the summer of 1917, following the failure of the 1916–17 potato harvest and the successful German submarine blockade on shipping, wrote:

…we never had no potatoes for nine months, but instead rice, rice three times a day, nearly at every meal the bisquits were all broken bits and full or worms or maggots, and

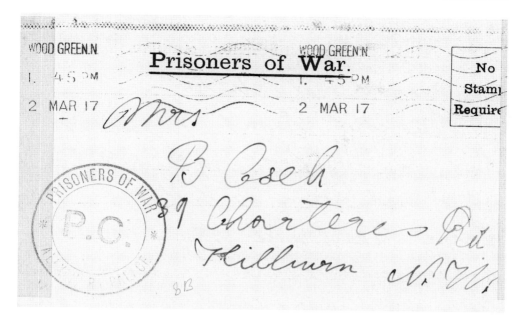

schwedes turnips, also twice salt herrings a week, but they were all foul so that no-one could eat them, we refused to have them but the Authoritys insisted that we should eat them. We found many with worms in them, we had some sent to Kensington Museum for Analisys and the report was that the worms were quite harmless, and we must eat them as the Authoritys will allow nothing else instead, but we refused and had to do without anything. I saw sixty-five barrels taken away on two motor lorries, all doomed to be buried, but at that time our wives were still allowed to bring us some food from outside on visiting days, or send parcels by post, but nearly every following month reductions in our rations took place and restrictions against wives were made. They were actually searched, theyr parcels for us confiscated and so fort. At last, everything was prohibited but apples and frish herrings. The Authoritys knew full well they could not be had … we received no butter or margarine. Dividing out [food] at the tables was no easy matter, and regular fights took place.

Unsurprisingly, as the rations reduced and the quality became ever poorer, the internees thought constantly of food. Paul Cohen-Portheim, writing from Wakefield internment camp, in *Time Stood Still*, recounts that:

One article of diet after another vanished. Horseflesh made its appearance (it tastes like very tough and sugary beef), vegetables disappeared. Bread was gritty and mouldy, then it disappeared altogether for months and was replaced by 'broken biscuit' which is just like pebbles. Potatoes were frozen and sickeningly sweet, then there were no potatoes at all. Milk went, butter went. One really always felt hungry, everybody's health suffered, people got ever thinner and ever more listless.

The *Daily Mail*, however, knew better than the internees. Part of an article of 1917 on internment, entitled 'Our Happy Huns' touched on the amount of food allowed to the prisoners daily. The article, in informing its hungry readers, alleged that:

> His meat ration is still twenty ounces a week (four ounces a day on each of five days) – far bigger than the British civilian's ration of one and fourpence worth of meat a week. On the other two days the Germans have twelve ounces of herrings. They have daily one pound of potatoes, twenty-three ounces of bread and green vegetables, peas, margarine, flour for pastry, rice, cheese and other foodstuffs. For breakfast they have bread, margarine, herrings and jam when available. Typical dinners for the five meat dinners are roast mutton, roast beef, Irish stew, boiled beef and a German meat dish with vegetables each day.

The death on 5 June 1916 of War Minister, Lord Kitchener (Kitchener of Khartoum – K of K), the adored war hero, inflamed anti-German feeling throughout Britain. With military deaths and injuries rising daily and all available institutions filled with the wounded, feelings again ran high. Local councillors began a campaign against the use of Alexandra Palace for the internees, wanting them thrown out and this 'healthful site' used for the deserving war-wounded. Conversely, other councillors cried 'Intern Them All!' Among these was Cllr Harvey. At a council meeting in June 1916, Cllr Harvey stated: 'There is no hardship in being interned. Not many miles away there is a camp where the interned have such conditions of life that there are thousands of people in Tottenham who would be glad to change places. Not only are these people being given the best food, but they have entertainment and are trained in wood carving and all sorts of things. So well provided are they that any bread as might be left from the weekend supply is sold to the people of Wood Green'. He felt sure the good people of Wood Green would feel most grateful to their German guests.

A small news item in the local papers of November 1916 was headed 'Fastidious Prisoners' and confirmed Rudolf Rocker's complaint about the hostile press. This reported that internees at Alexandra Palace had complained their sleep at night was disturbed by the tread of soldiers on duty. The complaint had reached the ears of MP Mr Nield, who asked in the House of Commons whether, in consequence of the complaint, coconut matting had been laid 'at considerable expense'. The reply stated that the noise of the sentries' tread was accentuated by the nature of the building, and wooden platforms above the prisoners' heads. The matting had been laid twelve months before. However, Rudolf Rocker, upon referring to the sentries' night duties, noted: '...it is not so very long ago that they were pacing hollow platforms in the barrack rooms, night and day, with heavy tread, to the general disturbance of the captives, and their own weariment. Sometimes one [a guard], overcome with sleep himself, would drop his rifle with a crash, and forthwith wake up a thousand sleeping men'.

A blow to the morale of the internees was the death of the Camp Commandant – Lt Col Frowde-Walker. An obituary in the *Wood Green Herald* of 25 July 1917 stated that he was 'a gentleman who commanded the respect and affection of all with whom he came in contact ... and was popular with the officers and men of the guard under his care'. The obituary does not mention the high esteem and affection in which he was held by

Above: *Preparing food for a meal.*

Below: *The food ration being portioned out.*

the internees. One internee, working in the hospital as an orderly, deferred his chance of release in order to nurse Lt Col Frowde-Walker until his death. His replacement, Lt Col Luscombe, had been transferred from the camp at Stratford in East London, from where he brought a far stricter regime to both internees and the military under his command. His threat of removal to the Isle of Man was usually sufficient to quell any dissidence.

Rudolf Rocker, again:

Internment generally is considered as a kind of Eldorado: theatrical entertainments, concerts, tennis and billiards are cited as commonplace. The amusements of a handful of better placed men appear to be the order of the day. In political campaigns the prisoners are further exploited with tales of the well-fed and pampered Hun. So, without consideration of their total rations a single item, such as margarine or jam is held up as proof of shameful extravagance on the part of this or that government department upon which rests the responsibility of feeding the prisoners, with the result that generally the item is deleted.

Recruitment drive 4 August 1916.

Rocker, referring to the wealthy residing in A Tower and other select locations within the Palace, but well away from the massed prisoners of the battalions, stated:

> With the help of all their money they buy all sorts of privileges, very often at the cost of the generality. And yet, such a one has it to the good that he is able, upon the strength of his financial means, even in captivity to purchase many comforts from which the large majority of prisoners are entirely excluded. The well known words of Philip of Macedonia that "No wall is so high as to be insurmountable to an ass laden with gold" retain their truth even in an internment camp.

W.R. Hughes writes of the better-placed prisoners who were ever ready to help out the less fortunate. One such worthy located in A Tower was internee M. Kastner who:

> …during the period of his internment Mr Kastner has acted as Chairman of the Doctor Märkel Committee and of the Arts and Handicrafts Committee, both of which have been doing valuable work among their fellow prisoners to the general benefit of the morale and discipline of the camp. Mr Kastner has always acted … in matters dealing with the relief of families of interned men of the camp who have been in distressed circumstances owing to various causes … [and] that he has personally assisted in a number of needy cases.

A further report written by W.R. Hughes in early January 1918 states that Mr Kastner had now left for internment in Holland, and refers to these Committees helping more men than ever before to find some occupation.

The *Wood Green Herald* of 14 December 1917 carried an item on one of the privileged men. This alleged that, 'following a question in the House of Commons, it had been revealed that a wealthy alien had been transferred from Alexandra Palace, under guard, to the Isle of Man, with his valet, secretary and excess luggage to a large amount'. The news item contrasted this with the widely held belief about the ill treatment meted out to British prisoners in German camps, concluding that: 'It is possible the servants were interned aliens also, but it is puzzling to understand how such a retinue can be maintained under the circumstances'.

In contrast to the wealthy men and those with recognised trades such as tailors or watchmakers, there were many who had no skills and, in the camp milieu were unemployable. These included waiters, stokers and sailors. The report of the Swiss Embassy of 14 March 1916 refered to these men as: '…really to be pitied because there is no way of occupying them for industrial, agricultural and other purposes. The greatest kindness one could do for these prisoners would be to find real work for them. This would be much more valuable to them than any amount of money given to them for charity's sake'.

Twenty-four deaths occurred in the first three months of 1919 at the Palace, with sometimes several funerals taking place on the same day. These were presumably caused by the influenza pandemic that killed millions worldwide.

A news item in the *Wood Green Herald* of 14 March 1919 stated that: 'There had been a good deal of influenza among the interned aliens at the Alexandra Palace. The hospital has been unusually full and there has, we believe, been a number of deaths'.

During the years of internment there were many deaths at the Palace, including suicides. Of the fifty-four deaths of Alexandra Palace internees recorded in the Burial Registers of the Great Northern Cemetery, Southgate, twenty-three of these occurred at the Colney Hatch Lunatic Asylum. No records have been discovered for other internee deaths – presumably the body was removed for private burial elsewhere. The majority were interred in common graves at the Great Northern Cemetery. The exception to this was Franz Erfurt (49) who died on 1 November 1915 and is buried in a private grave (R 1069) in the Great Northern. The grave, registered in the camp commandant's name, Lt Col Frowde-Walker, was intended for two people although Franz is the sole occupant. Just within the cemetery entrance stands a memorial to the Palace internees buried there.

Left: *Grave of Franz Erfurt inscribed 'Unserm kameraden Franz Erfurt; 23 Juni 1867 – 1 November 1915'.*

Below: *Memorial to internees at Great Northern Cemetery, Southgate.*

❧ NINE ❧

KILLING TIME

R udolf Rocker, in his diary from 1915, wrote:

> It was a splendid gathering of men which found itself in Alexandra Palace during 1915; and
> it stood in every respect higher than the generality of the present inmates of the camp. At
> that time there were present a large proportion of excellent teachers on all kinds of subjects,
> and when the Commandant placed at our disposal three rooms for studying purposes, there
> developed in a very short time, a rich mental life. Numerous classes for various sciences,
> and for the learning of foreign languages were founded; and these were attended by over
> 700 students. Besides these, scientific lectures took place which dealt with every conceivable
> subject. The teachers undertook their several tasks with love and devotion, and they were
> well compensated by the application of their pupils. In the course of six months there had
> grown up a little university which was the pride of the camp.

This was initially successful until it was decided that Alexandra Palace would be used as
a clearing house for those being repatriated. Rudolf Rocker describes the repatriation
scheme as a 'tragedy without end' for those forced to participate. With the constant
movements and disruption, the mental life of the camp destroyed, the school soon
collapsed.

In 1916, at a cost of £1,000, the YMCA proposed building a hut in the grounds that
could be used by the internees, surpassing all those built in other camps. An interned
architect designed the plan of the building and undertook technical supervision of the
construction. Initially there were sufficient volunteers to help with the building; it was
only later, when most of these had been sent to the Isle of Man, that their replacements
were paid a few shillings a week which was subscribed for, in the main, by the prisoners
themselves. On Christmas Day 1917 the new building was ready for use.

With plans made for use of the completed hut, the commandant then informed the prisoners the building could not be used after the evening count, which took place between 4.00 p.m. and 5.00 p.m. during the winter months, meaning the rooms could only be used during the day for studies. Rudolf Rocker wrote:

> But it is just the winter months which are best suited for studying and mental occupations generally; as during this season the prisoners must feel the irksome and hopeless monotony of their internment doubly.
>
> An embitterment was created, not so easily be stamped out; and this worked the deepest as the men knew that in other camps the YMCA huts could be used until 9.00 p.m. Besides this, many of them had read in the English press of the YMCA at Ruhleben.

This had been in existence since 1915 and the interned English civilians had instituted a small university, with facilities to study and take degrees at British universities.

Rocker adds:

> And there stands a finished building, well furnished and specially erected for this purpose, but it cannot be used because a forceful military order, which contravenes all common sense, forbids them from doing so. And withal, this unreasonable order cannot in any way be justified. The building is situated within the barbed wire entanglements … the only explanation for such a groundless action is the absolute lack of comprehension for the real position of the captives. But it is just the senselessness of such a restriction which creates much bad blood. If the authorities had only the slightest notion of how detrimental such an order works, how much embitterment it creates, and to what depths it influences the mentality of the prisoners, they would, God knows!, be more careful.

On the subject of work, Rudolf Rocker wrote:

> To distract the thoughts of the prisoners at least to some extent − there is only one way, namely − to work. Although the majority of the captives are entirely without means, it would be wrong to assume that remuneration plays the chief part with them. Neither is it the inner natural necessity for work which prompts his resolve. The more the prisoner finds opportunity to satisfy his active instincts, the more he is helped to overcome the monotony of the creeping hours, days and weeks.

Some prisoners found work in their former occupations, being re-engaged by their old employers working in their trades, mainly watchmakers and die-sinkers. The men received trade-union rates, from which the government deducted 2s 6d weekly for their keep. Other men found employment with the Alexandra Palace Trust, some as gardeners while others maintained the Palace's roads and paths. Each received 4s 6d per week.

For those men of no particular talent or skill, the hours hung heavily. Before his death Lt Col Frowde-Walker experimented with giving interested prisoners a small plot of land which each could cultivate to his own taste. At first, only about eighty men could obtain such an allotment. The experiment was such a success that the following year over 400

Allotments on the Palace's eastern front.

plots were given to the men, but again supply outstripped demand. Busy the whole day through in their gardens, what was achieved was remarkable. Some cultivated flowers, while others grew vegetables.

Rudolf Rocker observed that:

> The gloomy and tired expression, which is so characteristic of captivity, has completely gone from their faces, and given place to a mien more free from care. No other work had so beneficial an influence as this, and it is only to be regretted that it cannot come into question during the long winter months. Nothing acts so mildly and tranquillisingly upon the psychological condition of the prisoners as the occupation in the open nature, surrounded by flowers and plants which they tended and brought to growth with their own hands, and although it is not able to resign them to their loss, it helps them greatly to overcome more easily the hopeless, creeping monotony of captivity.

In September 1915, the *Konzert Verein* was founded, in which most of the interned musicians participated. Following its foundation weekly concerts were given in the theatre, usually on Sunday evenings, and were greatly appreciated by the prisoners. Music and musical instruments were provided by Dr Märkel's Committee.

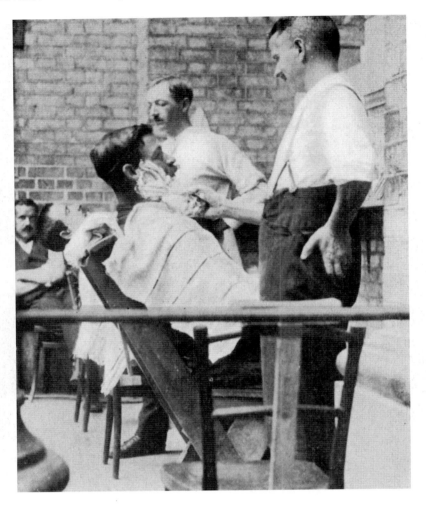

Barbers at work.

The first concert, for 'A' and 'B' Battalions, took place on 19 September at 6.30 p.m. in the theatre, with the same concert repeated on 20 September for 'C' Battalion. The music chosen was all Germanic in origin with the orchestra conducted by Anton Würst. The second concert on 3 October featured bass singer Herr Lino Vesco and violin virtuoso F. Lorant, plus a choir. The concerts continued, often several times weekly until Alexandra Palace's closure, always featuring high quality performers from among the internees, many of whom were professional musicians in their homelands. Amateur musicians were also encouraged to attend daily rehearsals.

A blow to the orchestra was the death of its Austrian conductor, Gustave Wanda, aged forty. He had been interned at Alexandra Palace since August 1915, where he became ill. Taken to the German Hospital in Dalston, he underwent surgery but never recovered and died in December 1915.

Unknown members of the camp orchestra.

He was renowned in Europe where, for eight years, he had been conductor in Berlin's Winter Gardens. Before his internment he had been offered a large salary to go to the United States to conduct a light opera of his own composition. Permission for him to travel had been given but arrived a few hours after his death.

Facilities were provided for internees to undertake hobbies at their own expense, the men being encouraged to take up handicrafts. Woodworking, carving ox bones into ornaments, marquetry, toy-making and art (paintings, drawing etc.) all flourished. In Battalions 'A' and 'B' at Alexandra Palace the workspace, which was wholly inadequate for the number of men wishing to occupy themselves, was part of the barrack rooms where the internees lived and slept. So the men moved their activities to their bedsides which at first was forbidden but eventually the authorities had to give way. The location of the workshops and the working between the beds meant the whole camp was constantly filled

Tailors at work.

Internees making models and toys.

with noises of hammering, sawing, filing, and so on. This was extremely detrimental to the mental health of the prisoners, especially during the long winter months, when forced to remain indoors by bad weather and early head counts.

The lighting of the camp was entirely inadequate. The few gas lamps seldom burned brightly – the quality and pressure of the gas being reduced and various economy schemes practised – so the light they provided did little to keep up the spirits of the men interned. To read meant risking ruined eyesight, for those strong enough to concentrate their thoughts in such an atmosphere. In a single enclosed space where men have to eat, sleep, work and occupy their leisure, the mutual disturbances could destroy every occupation or thought. Rocker wrote: 'So it happens that the activities of one part of the prisoners hinders, and in many cases makes entirely impossible, that of the others. This unfortunate condition causes a whole series of constant frictions in the camp, and develops among many of the interned a high graded nervousness, which becomes ever more unbearable as the captivity continues. More especially the older men suffer from this'. Rocker continued:

> The unceasing noise of the camp is a source of constant suffering, which periodically brings men near desperation. It did not seldom happen that elderly gentlemen came to me with tears in their eyes, and complained of this torture. So I ordered then at least that, during hours between two and four in the afternoon, all noisy occupations should cease. That was all I could do under such a condition of things, but even this small measure failed often, owing to the inconsiderateness of single individuals.

Organised activities beyond the concerts frequently failed, both through lack of organisers and participants. The Amateur Theatre Society ceased its activities. The audiences to lectures and concerts dwindled, while organisations with a sporting aim, such as the *Turn Verein* (Gymnastic Association), the football club and others, also ceased eventually, mostly through apathy induced by long internment and malnutrition from food restrictions. Gambling flourished, especially among young German born boys interned at the age of seventeen. Encouraged to the tables by older experienced gamblers, many soon became addicted. Rocker stated:

> The pulse beat of the camp has no more the same vitality which it had in former days, and the standard of the prisoners has in every way deteriorated. When formerly men occupied themselves with games, gymnastics, theatrical performances and the like, we now come upon listless groups, idly standing about, without energy or initiative for anything.

The only entertainment that flourished and grew was the *kino* (cinema), which had begun in 1915. Starting with one weekly performance which then grew to two weekly, Rudolf Rocker observed that:

> In his thoughts he lives in the landscape that passes before his eyes; he mingles with the crowds at the railway station, boards ships and trains, and takes personal part in the dramas that take place before him. What the fairy tale is to the child, that is the 'kino' to the prisoner.

Arts and Handicraft Committee members. Among those seen here are Tomitz, Schecker, Strecker, Ficker, Brandes, Kastuer and Herzog.

Despite privations within Alexandra Palace, there were men who managed to rise above their surroundings and use their time creatively. Among these were Dr Henry S. Simonis, whose monograph *Zum Alten Jüdischen Zivil Recht* was written while he was interned at the Palace and published in Berlin in 1922.

Another was artist Rudolf Sauter, interned at Alexandra Palace from 1918 to 1919, together with his father Professor Georg Sauter, a professional artist and Secretary of the International Society. Rudolf Sauter's images, in pen and ink and wash reflected the monotony and far from luxurious conditions at Alexandra Palace. Most of Sauter's works are now in private collections.

Upon his release, Rudolf Sauter did not follow an artistic career, but instead became secretary to the novelist John Galsworthy, inheriting a share in Galsworthy's royalties, which made him financially independent. He died in 1979.

Rudolf's father, who had spent twenty years in England before being interned, was so disgusted at his treatment that upon repatriation to Germany he never visited England again.

❧ TEN ❧

HUN WIVES

Rudolf Rocker wrote of the wives and children of the interned men: 'Here also I cannot refrain from expressing an intense admiration for the large majority of the wives of the interned, for they have stood nobly by their husbands in the direct misfortune, very often they have suffered, regardless of poverty the ostracism of "friends" and relatives and even parents, besides the insults of thoughtless misguided multitudes rather than forsake their men'. He continues: 'When Belgian families whose homes were destroyed fled from their invaded land, they were received as refugees and victims of the war. Pity and hospitality were extended to them. But to these thousands here, even though their wives and children were of British birth, and though many of their sons are in the armies of the Allies – mere justice was not shown to them. They are made prisoners and taunted as "Huns"'.

There were cases where women were not able to withstand public opinion or where their former life was so unhappy it could not bear the strain, but these were believed to be relatively rare.

One anti-German society approached many of the wives with offers of assistance to obtain divorces. On the lines that he was a hated German, some cases were successful in seducing the wife away from loyalty to her man.

At visits the prisoner had to hear stories of indignities and want, misery and illness with which his family had to bear, of parents casting off their daughters for having married a man born overseas. Often these stories were told under the masks of forced gaiety and 'humour', but served only to cover appearances, and were unable to hide the true state of affairs. All this emphasised the prisoners' inability to raise a hand in their defence.

Among the family parties visiting a prisoner were occasionally sons, some wounded, serving in the Allied armies or navies, coming to visit their interned father or brothers. Rudolf Rocker asked: 'What is the psychology of the father, whose son is braving the dangers and hardships of war, while he himself is looked on as an enemy to the very country his son is fighting for?' He continued: 'What must the mental state of a mother be, whose husband is interned and whose boy is risking life and limb in the cause of those who have declared his father their enemy, while she herself is classed as an alien enemy in the country of her birth?'

Local newspapers reported many stories of the wives of aliens. Through ignorance, many found themselves in a police court for the first time in their lives. In one case the bench learned that the defendant was the widow of a German who had died four years before.

Alderman Huggett asked her: 'You became a German citizen on marriage?' She retorted: 'Oi was born in Oireland in the City of Cark'. Alderman Huggett replied: 'No further evidence is needed as to her original place of birth'. The bench learned that she had complied with the registration and discharged her.

Another defendant appeared before the court, a widow born of English parents, whose German husband lived in England for twenty-seven years and had applied for naturalisation just before his death. Their son was in the British Army and the prisoner had never been out of England. The offence was committed out of ignorance. She was bound over for six months.

Newspapers carried the story: 'A German wife's dilemma'. In defence of the woman, her counsel pleaded that she not be deported as she had no connection with Germany, saying: 'It is a most uncommon thing for a German woman to be interned. Practically, it has never been done'. The Judge, Sir Robert Wallace KC, replied: 'That is exactly what I want to know something about. I should have thought that many German women were just as dangerous as German men and ought to be interned'. Judgement was postponed so the Home Office could be contacted.

A wife from south London, whose husband was interned at Alexandra Palace from May 1915, was charged on remand of abandoning her male child, aged four weeks. The story in the *Forest Hill, Sydenham and Penge Examiner* of 22 September 1916 reported that the English-born woman, who was German through marriage, deposited the baby on a doorstep in Belgravia at 10.30 p.m. on 9 September and very shortly afterwards it was discovered by a servant residing next door. In the course of a statement, she said: 'It was nice and warm when I left it on the step, wrapped in two shawls and covered with an old shirt, thinking some lady who could better afford to keep it would pick it up. I tried to get it into a home but had no money to advertise it. With four other children I can't face another winter like the last one'. The baby had been taken to Westminster Infirmary. Almost immediately after abandoning the baby she attended Catford police station to report what she had done. The court remanded her in custody for a week for further enquiries.

She told the court she was in receipt of 18s 6d per week from the Poor Law Guardians for herself and her four children. The money was not sufficient so she had been working illegally as a barmaid, leaving her situation because of her illegitimate child.

Shortly after the sinking of the *Lusitania* and following the anti-German riots, Sylvia Pankhurst referred to these women in her publication *The Women's Dreadnought*: '…shall we revenge ourselves on other helpless people who are living in our midst and who are no more to blame either for the sinking of the *Lusitania* of for the war itself, than we ourselves?'

Sylvia Pankhurst described:

> …a Poplar woman, an English woman by birth, a good woman, who has done much voluntary work and made many a little sacrifice for people poorer than herself, who is married to a German who has lived peaceably and honestly in this country for many years. On Tuesday night her home was wrecked, all the furniture, everything that she had, even the very tools with which her industrious son and husband earned their living as cabinet makers were taken away. Her husband, her young son and her daughter disappeared. She came to us distracted, having seen her husband, son and daughter dragged out of the house by the mob, she could find no trace of her dear ones, she knew not whether they were killed or injured'. A day of agonised suspense elapsed before they were able to rejoin her.
>
> A neighbour, as English as herself, married to a German, passed through the same terrible experience: and in fear and grief was prematurely confined, alone in the empty house, with only the bare boards left on which to lay herself.

Sylvia Pankhurst concluded: 'This is not patriotism. It is cowardice to abuse these people and plunder the homes of those who are too weak to defend themselves. Let us not be cowards'.

Families were already suffering long before the sinking of the *Lusitania*. In many cases, they had been evicted from their homes, their men having lost their jobs. For example, an Austrian night porter aged twenty-nine who lived in New Eltham with his pregnant wife and child. He was interned on 10 February 1915 after applying for a police permit to visit the Emergency Committee of the Society of Friends in Central London to obtain assistance.

Extracts from correspondence about this family include the following: '…as the man was not in employment at the time of his internment … the committee offered to admit the woman and child to their institution [workhouse], pending the mother's accouchement, which is expected shortly'. Another letter, referring to them, stated that:

> These Guardians (Lewisham Workhouse) refuse to give relief to this woman and her child and only offer them the workhouse. As it is well known, the majority of interned aliens lost their employment from causes due to the war before being interned … the price of food and fuel have risen considerably so that the scale fixed in November [1914] no longer suffices to maintain the recipients [of relief] even at the minimum physical efficiency … as regards the particular case mentioned, we understand that the Guardians have considered it desirable for the wife to be received into the infirmary [workhouse] and she has agreed to go there.

The allowance to English-born wives was handled by the local Poor Law Guardians and was worded: 'they may give up to such and such an amount if deemed necessary'. Thus the payment of a grant in any given case was left at the option of the Local Poor Law Guardians. To establish a claim the English-born alien had to produce proof of her English birth, her marriage certificate and proof of her husband's internment. Many people sold or pawned everything they could before applying to the Guardians. Then it often took weeks before the requirements of the Guardians could be met.

No Government grants were given until November 1914, not until several weeks after the men had been interned. The scale at first fixed was: 'up to ten shillings per week' for the wife and 1s 6d for each child under the age of fourteen. Country cases received far less. In the London area, Wimbledon was considered to be 'country'.

On May 19 1915, after considerable persuasion, the Government raised the grant in the London area to 11s 6d per week, and 1s 9d for each child aged under fourteen. Finally, on 19 February 1917, the grants in the London area were increased to 12s 6d for the wife and 3s for each child under fourteen. The country grant was raised at the same time to 10s for the wife and 3s for each child.

Guardians constantly threatened to reduce or stop these grants, while others did whenever the woman was able to earn a small sum, no matter how occasionally the woman was able to obtain work.

An official visitor from St Stephen's House had been asked to talk to one of the alien wives, suggesting better way of how to manage her £1 2s a week allowance. The woman had six children, the eldest a boy of twelve. The woman's weekly expenses were:

Rent	7s 6d
Bread	7s 6d
Gas	1s 0d
Fuel	1s 0d
Insurance★	0s 6d
Pieces of shoe leather	1s 0d
Various	1s 0d
TOTAL	19s 6d

[★Insurance – this was burial insurance because the shame of a pauper's funeral was something a family, no matter how impoverished, found unbearable.]

The official concluded that, 'After these were paid there remained only two shillings and sixpence for all other food [for the week], and I failed to find a way by which she could do without the Committee's (St Stephen's House) grant of a pint of milk a day'. (A report of the Friends' (Quakers) Emergency Work in England 1914-20 p.87).

In this case, as in so many others, the amount of bread purchased equalled the cost of the weekly rent. Bread, sold by weight, was the staple diet of the very poor, with many families having bread for breakfast, bread at midday and bread for supper. Bread was filling, cheap, ready cooked, portable and adaptable. If there was sufficient money, it was served perhaps with a scraping of margarine or, as a treat, a farthingsworth of jam or a ha'porth of dripping, the nearest many families got to meat. Tea, if affordable, would be a half-penny's worth wrapped in a screw of newspaper with the leaves brewed and re-brewed until they were tasteless.

Boots and items of clothing were impossible to purchase at this level of subsistence, so many organisations, such as The Salvation Army and societies such as St Stephen's House, provided these free of charge.

Another case among the thousands with which St Stephen's House dealt was that of an English woman whose German husband, a former waiter, was interned from 1914–19. At the outbreak of war there were six children in the family; the youngest died of pneumonia and poverty during the war. The mother, suffering from persistent attacks of pleurisy, half starved and badly overworked managed to keep the others alive, although the children showed signs of severe malnutrition. The children depended upon their daily, free school dinner until these were stopped by the authorities on the grounds that the children of alien enemies were forbidden free school meals. The woman lived in terror of being called in front of the Guardians, which she endured every few weeks, to show cause why the Government grant should not be stopped for, as an able-bodied woman she should be able to find work.

In a letter published in *The Times* of 23 August 1917, author Arthur Conan Doyle, the President of the Divorce Law Reform Union, quoted cases of British-born women married to Germans and proposed that they be allowed to divorce.

An 'American Wife of an English Husband' responded thus in *The Times* of 25 August 1917: 'English wives of Germans took their husbands "for better for worse, till death do us part" and that no amount of inconvenience caused by the contract can justify their declaring it to be a scrap of paper which necessity compels them to destroy'.

The indignities endured by these women, and directed with equal venom towards their children, came not only from official sources but, in some instances, from their close relatives, neighbours and former friends, as well as from the public and authorities. Unable to travel outside their neighbourhood for a distance further than five miles, unable to move to a different location, unable to revert to their maiden names, unable to work in a time of booming employment for women, they were forced into the workhouse, or penury, by trying to live on the meagre allowances administered by the local Poor Law Union, which carefully watched every penny doled out. The following accounts are far from rare.

The Poor Law Union for Cockermouth, Cumbria, had several British-born wives of interned alien enemies on their books. All the men were imprisoned by the end of the December quarter 1914.

One woman of Flimby, Cumbria, whose husband was interned at Knockaloe on the Isle of Man, had three children and, at the start of the war was entitled to 12s 6d per week, comprising 8s for the wife and 1s 6d per child. This was their sole income, which grew incrementally until by 1917 the family were entitled to 19s per week. The death of her small daughter on 5 July 1917 reduced the weekly income by 3s to 16s. From the week immediately following the little girl's death she received the new amount, and thus it stayed until the release of her husband in May 1919.

It may be assumed that, living in small communities life was difficult for these women and their children. Part of a letter dated 20 April 1916 from the Relieving Officer of the Poor Law Union says that in the case of a woman from Great Clifton, whose husband was interned in Alexandra Palace before removal to Knockaloe, was entitled to relief of 1s 9d weekly for her two children, with nothing for herself. By September 1916 this sum had increased to 5s to the end of March 1917, before increasing to 16s until 1919 when her husband was released.

Others who came under the care of the Cockermouth Poor Law Union included a woman from Keswick, whose husband had been interned at Libury Hall at Ware in Hertfordshire. Another Keswick woman's husband was interned at Alexandra Palace, and a woman of Workington's husband was repatriated via Rotterdam in May 1919, after internment on the Isle of Man, ending up in a German military camp by November 1919.

The Poor Law Union for Strood in Kent had only three British-born wives on its books.

One was Ellen Turk, my great-aunt. Her husband Carl (Charlie) had arrived in Britain as a toddler around 1871. The family had broken off all contact with Germany, and made themselves as English as possible. Therefore great-uncle Charlie grew up in East London as a typical 'Cockney Sparrer'. A dapper man and nimble dancer, he had worked his way up from labourer to foreman by the time of the birth of his second child, Olive, in May 1914. He married in 1908, had a good job, a wife and family and resided at Sea Belle

Carl 'Charlie' Turk (37) and Ellen Gill (21) on their wedding day, 16 May 1908.

Villa in a semi-detached house, adjacent to Rosherville Park in Northfleet, Kent; pleasant surroundings with views of the Thames. They were comfortably off, had a well-furnished home and Charlie, being a thrifty man, savings and a secure future.

Following the sinking of the *Lusitania* in May 1915, Gravesend and the surrounding area erupted into violence. While the focus of the riots appeared to be German-sounding businesses in the centre of Gravesend, and known German residents, this was the event that triggered Great-Uncle Charlie's arrest and internment on 23 July 1915, He was taken directly to Alexandra Palace, becoming prisoner 17526, where he remained until his release in July 1919.

Left with a small boy of two, and a baby of one year, Ellen was provided with a weekly income from the Board of Guardians of 10s. Unable to manage, she moved in with her parents.

As an old man in his eighties, their son, Chaz, (Charles) recalled going to Alexandra Palace with his mother for visits. Once the official visit was over he and his mother would walk into the grounds and wait at a pre-arranged spot for a further meeting. While husband and wife conversed through the heavy rolls of barbed wire, Chaz would play with the latest toy his father had made him. Having no idea of the circumstances behind the visits Chaz confessed just before his death that it was the lure of a new toy, rather than seeing his father, that was the attraction. He said the sound of orchestral music was always intertwined with his memories of the Palace.

Released from Frimley camp in July 1919, after the signing of the Treaty of Versailles, Charlie returned home. An outcast in the town, told in no uncertain terms by his previous employers that they didn't employ Huns and unable to find other work apart from occasional navvying, he suffered a fall and died of broncho-pneumonia in February 1923 aged 52. He was interred in Northfleet Cemetery on 10 February. Ellen was also buried in the same grave in August 1965.

While his son had recollections of his father, his daughter Olive could not remember him at all. The only mementoes she had of him were a marquetry matchbox cover and a hand mirror for Ellen, decorated on the back with blue forget-me-nots and inscribed 'Nelly'.

Small as were the allowances given to the British-born wives, those administered to foreign-born women and their families were even scantier, and they were required to sign a promise that they would repay after the war any allowance given. Many women, knowing they could never repay the money, did not apply for the allowance at all.

The distress of the British-born wives and families was nationwide. An appeal for money was published in the *Manchester Guardian* of 30 September 1916 from the Society for the Relief of Distressed Foreigners. The Society alleged that since the beginning of the war they had paid about £20,000 to people who had reached the end of their resources and dealt with over one thousand individual cases.

The letter continues: 'We have on our books the names of some two hundred British-born women whose husbands are interned, and whose totally inadequate Local Government Board [weekly] allowance of nine shillings and threepence for themselves and one-shilling and ninepence for each child, we are obliged to support. For obvious reasons it is impossible for aliens to find work'.

...........*Slooad*...........*Union.*

Form C.
(Class C.)

British-Born Wives and Children of Interned Aliens.

Statement of cost of assistance given to wives and children of interned aliens during the quarter ended on *30ᵗʰ September* 1919.

(The reason for any money payment in excess of the authorised scale rate should be stated on the claim, in accordance with the memorandum of 3rd July, 1918.)

Name of interned alien.	Nationality (insert G. or A.)	Date of internment.	If not still interned, date and cause of release.	Number of dependent children.	Period of assistance. From	To	Weekly rate. s. d.	Number of Weeks.	Total Cost. £ s. d.
	2	3	4	10	11	12	13	14	15
		1919			1919	1919			
Turk Charles	G	23.7.15	July	2	July 1	July 15	10 -	2	1. 0. 0
Blesch Johannes Gottlieb Daniel	G	11.9.14	*	3	July 1	Sep 30	5.7½	39 3/7	11. 1. 9

* Mr. Blesch was repatriated some three years ago and the Guardians will be glad if the children can now be returned to the care of their father in Germany

Total **12. 1. 9**

I CERTIFY that to the best of my knowledge and belief the particulars included in the above

Sheet from the Poor Law Union showing payments to Ellen Turk, the date of Charles's internment and his release in 1919.

Further on, the letter stated that:

The English wives of enemy aliens themselves rank as enemy aliens and, having lost their English citizenship, it is this society they have to turn to when they are without private resources and friends. The helpless women and children who are of enemy nationality also have nowhere else to go except the workhouse in case of need. The German and Austrian governments make allowances (which are paid through the Local Government Board) in respect of their subjects, but these fall far short of providing adequate subsistence. The consequent privation is serious, and the lack of sufficient nourishment is leaving a trail of weakness and disease, particularly tuberculosis.

The letter then cites a few cases, including:

…that of an English born wife of a German with six children, the eldest of whom is fourteen. Her husband, who was a waiter in Southport, has been interned. Southport is in a prohibited area and she has now been warned to leave. Probably she will come to Manchester. She received through the Local Government Board an allowance of eighteen shillings per week, and she earns a few shillings by charring. The rent she has had to pay in Southport, is ten shillings per week. She has no relations.

There is Scottish wife of an interned alien is lying on her deathbed, suffering from cancer. She has two little boys and her income is the twelve shillings and ninepence she receives from the Local Government Board.

There are two Galicean families [then part of the Austrian Empire]. The father of one was turned out of Swansea, which is a prohibited area, and the wife and seven children settled in Manchester. The husband is now in an asylum. In the other family there are nine children. The father, a tailor, came to this country when a boy. He has no papers to prove his nationality and has no allowances from the Austrian government. He can earn very little, and the maintenance of the whole family falls to a large extent on the Society for the Relief of Distressed Foreigners. An Alsatian with a wife and seven children claims that he is a Frenchman because he was born before 1870, when Alsace was French territory, but he is officially classed as a German. He is ailing and can only work occasionally, and one of the children is consumptive.

The letter ends with an appeal for funds to continue the work, asking that all donations be sent to the Manchester County Bank or to the Chairman of the Special War Distress Committee, Mr F. Zimmern at No. 21 Lime Grove, Manchester.

Mrs E. Hancke of Hoxton, East London, wrote to the Board of Guardians thus:

Sir, I beg to draw your attention to my case. I went last Thursday to Hoxton House for my allowance and they refused to give me any money for myself and my three children because I have been doing some work to keep and clothe my family and pay ten shillings and sixpence rent. As you must know yourself, we cannot live on the money and the cost of living is dear. Sir, my work is not regular. I am an old woman and I do a day or more when sent for. I have not been since last Wednesday as my baby had blood poisoin [sic] left from the flu and I have also had a lot of illness with my other children which costs money for a doctor. I have worked and paid for it, which I could not do out of my allowance.

Sir, I do not ask you to keep me, I only want to support my children as I have to pay for them to be looked after when I am at work. One is four years, one is five and the other is nine years, so you see they are quite young. Trusting you will grant me assistance for my children till the government send my husband home. Oblige me.

Mrs E. Hancke.

P.S. Please answer this letter as soon as possible.

A note of the bottom of the letter reads: 'Receives allowance of twenty-four shillings and sixpence and small sum for son in the army. Reported to be at work earning between eighteen and twenty-four shillings a week. Letter from employer gave average earnings of between twenty to twenty-two shillings per week'.

There is no evidence that Mrs Hancke received her money. Her letter, written on 10 November 1918, the day after the Armistice was signed, was also probably late in arriving at its destination, for the next day – 11 November – at the eleventh hour of the eleventh month, Armistice celebrations began.

❧ ELEVEN ❧

GOING HOME

Richard Notschke was repatriated on 16 February 1918. He wrote:

We had to give up our havy luggage next morning and leave the Palace at eight o'clock on the 16th. We wished to say goodbye to our wives, but as we had no visits until next week, we applied that very evening for a special permit to see our wives. It was granted and a special letter was sent to each one of them, and glad to say they all turned up the next afternoon. It was a sad day for all of us as no one knew if they would ever see them again. It was a very sad farewell but at the same time the thought of freedom overshadowed everything. We were going to be transferred to Spalding (Links) a small town on the East Coast. Here was errected a small camp in an old workhouse, the idea was that we should be sepparated from all other persons so we could devoulge no secrets.

After a breakfast of tea and two potatoes he said:

We left the Palace at six o'clock in the morning, about 185 of us, entrained at the Palace station and went down to King's Cross main line, here we changed trains, a strong military escort with us. Many persons were at the station and severall used very nasty remarks towards us. About nine o'clock the train started and off we went to Spalding in locked carriages and closely guarded with fixed bayonetts. It was two o'clock when we arrived in Spalding – the public all gazed at us as if we were some wild beasts. We were all driven into a small courtyard, counted names and numbers called, and then divided into twenty-one men in one room. I came on to the topmost floor. Here were strawsacks on the bare floor, each covered with three blankets, all very filthy and nasty looking, as good many men had slept on them before. We put down our belongings and then received our dinner, also our rations for the day – one ounce jam, one ounce sugar, five ounces bread and four ounces bisquits.

We were allowed to walk about a small garden; so it went on for three days.

Our heavy luggage had been sent on and on the third day detectives came from London to examine our luggage and ourselves. Each man was allowed a change of washing, but all other government articles of any kind were taken from us, also private new articles and all papers except the direct personal documents [such as] military passport and birth certificates. All our heavy luggage was then sealed. Next came the body examination. Each man had to stripp some more, some less, all were searched if they had papers or money on them, everything was turned out. No one was allowed to take more than £10 in money with them, but it was direct changed for a check on Cook's Bank in Amsterdam, so that no one could buy anything on the journey. Only a few odd shillings were left to each one. Before we were bodily examined we were driven from our room into another and then the military guard searched our room and after we had gone through our ordeal, we were driven back into out room again and then the doors were locked. Only at meal times we were escorted under strong guard to the dining and so back again, so that we should not speak to any other person, but there was no W.C. in or near the room and no arrangements had been made by those in charge, so we twenty-one men had to use the coal scuttle. The rest you can fairly well guess.

Our books and playing cards had been taken away, we had absolutely nothing we could pass our time away with, so we were sitting on strawsacks and telling each other stories and our experiences during the years of internment.

At last the day came that would set us free. Great was our joy when on 23 February we made a start to be transferred to Boston (Links) and from there to the ship. After a lot of preliminary we started off at about half past ten to the station, to be once more entrained, always our guards with fixed bayonetts with us. After a short journey we arrived at Boston Harbour, a small fishing place. Here that train stopped alongside the jetty, we had to remain in that train for nearly an hour. All our heavy luggage was thrown out of the luggage vans and so fearfull handled by those in charge of it. Old men, young men, soldiers, all acted as porters for us, we only looked on from the train. They broke most of the boxes, and smashed them against each other in such blind fury as was never experienced before, actually playing football with the lighter articles. The officials, and the officers who had escorted us, looked silently on. Several of our men protested but it was of no use, many articles were by then hanging out of their boxes and trunks, but they were all mercilessly thrown down a shippway on to a waiting tug. At last we were let off our train one by one. Everyone had to go before the port deportation official give his name and number once more and was then allowed to pass on to the waiting steam tug.

He concludes this passage:

After about one hour journey up the long creek we came to the open sea and could see three large ships about six miles from shore which had been provided by the Dutch government through the action of the Red Cross, all snow white painted and a broad red band painted right round the whole ship. As we got nearer was could see theyr names. It was the SS *Kölngin Regentes*, the *Lindora* and the *Zeeland*. Our tug steered direct for the *Kölngin Regentes*. We were soon alongside and the cheers went up from the whole party, answered

Head count of internees at Alexandra Palace prior to repatriation, 1919, as depicted by interned artist Rudolf Sauter.

by the waving handkershifs from those on board. It took very little time, and the whole party was transferred and the luggage thrown on board and the military guard who had escorted us all the way with fixed bayonets were left on the tug. At last we were free. Free so far that we could go about the ship wherever we pleased, no barbed wire here, no more bayonetts and no more insults. We were served dinner; a meal which everyone agreed was the best they had had since internment.

Luggage of repatriates being loaded onto lorry at Alexandra Palace, 1919, as depicted by interned artist Rudolf Sauter.

After waiting for the two other ships to load their parties of internees and enduring bad weather, eventually they set off a few days later. Battling the weather and aware of the threat of mines, the three ships stayed in close convoy as they steamed through the minefields. The lifeboats were ready – hanging over the sides should the ship be struck by a mine, each internee staying near their allocated position. Once notified, the ships were out of danger, Notschke reports that dinner was served then began 'all kinds of Jollyfication', arriving in Rotterdam later that night. The German Consul and his staff from Rotterdam came on board, the men were closely questioned, having to show proof of identity and were then allocated a free travel pass.

The next morning a reception party, including the Red Cross, welcomed the internees in the name of the Dutch nation. Upon disembarkation, the men were taken by train to the German border where they were again closely questioned before being given a free railway pass. Those who could not confirm their German origins were detained for further investigations.

Richard Notschke slept the night at the railway station before making his way to his brother's home in Elberfeld-Somborn. He stated: 'I arrived at my brother's home in the afternoon and that after twenty-seven years absence. It took from Alexander Palace fourteen days – the most eventful journey of my life'.

Writing from Elberfeld-Somborn in January 1920 Richard Notschke describes raging inflation, shortages, strikes, riots and slaughter. He wrote: 'In the very near future will be the election for the new Reichstag ... the outlook for the future is dark. The news arrived that peace has been ratified in Paris, twenty-six nations on one side, and Germany on the other, so this ends the terrible war'.

❧ TWELVE ❧

AFTERMATH

Armistice Day – 11 November 1918.

Buckingham Palace on a grey November morning, the roads muddy, the lake in St James's Park drained and full of huts. Lorries and motor cars were filled to overflowing with people, shouting for the King and singing the National Anthem, added to the general hubbub. The vast space in front of the Palace was occupied by a vaster crowd. The Victoria Memorial was thick with climbers swarming to its very top. 'We – want – King – George' was the cry, eventually the windows of the central balcony were flung open and the King, Queen, Princess Mary, the Duke of Connaught and Princess Patricia appeared, to the accompaniment of loud cheers. The King was observed to be laughing heartily. The Queen waved a Union Jack over her head. Accompanied by the massed bands of the Guards in the forecourt of the Palace, the crowd sang *Land of Hope and Glory*.

Children clambered over the captured German guns in the Mall, medical students bore aloft on a pole a skull labelled '*Hoch der Kaiser!*' Bonfires were made, the one at the base of Nelson's Column leaving permanent scarring on the stonework. Maroons on police and fire stations were let off and boy scouts on bicycles blew the 'All clear' on their trumpets for the last time, while factory and ships' hooters joined in the din.

The bells of Westminster Abbey and Westminster Cathedral rang in unison. Crowds were everywhere in the West End, draped in Union Jacks and the French tricolour. For those in Whitehall and Parliament Square the noise was stilled as Big Ben's chimes rang out for the first time in four years. When the hands of the dials pointed to XII, Big Ben struck the hour. As the last chime died away, the crowd burst into shouts of joy and singing

Despite the rain, which began to fall in the early afternoon, the crowds were undeterred that evening. They saw a searchlight display in the West End. Big Ben was illuminated, shops, public houses, theatres, cinemas and music halls were lit up, while workmen went around ripping the coverings from street lights. Trams, buses and trains also displayed lighted interiors. When the last revellers trudged home, they left behind a London many had feared never seeing again.

Outside London the West End celebrations were muted. Yellow envelopes containing the telegraphed regrets of the Army Council on the death of a male relative were still being delivered and there were thousands more to be sent. On Armistice Day alone 1,000 people died of Spanish Flu. As the lights went up, blinds signifying mourning were going down.

For the residents of Hornsey the Armistice was a low-key event. The *Hornsey Journal* of 18 November 1918 reported the muted response to Armistice Day as: 'When, at eleven o'clock, maroons were discharged at the police station and sirens sounded, some people prepared to take cover in case the worst happened. But when the bugles sounded the "All clear" and a distant heavy gun sounded a Royal salute all doubts were set aside'. Many people visited their local churches for thanksgiving services while, as the day wore on and despite the persistent rain, gradual realisation of the war's end took hold. Businesses closed for the day, school children were released from lessons, bunting and other decorations appeared in the streets and on buses and trams. Not wanting to waste a moment of their unexpected freedom, schoolboys soon set bonfires and released long-hoarded fireworks. Fairy lights and Chinese lanterns appeared in the windows of homes but it was not until the following night (Tuesday) that people began promenading in the newly lit streets: 'Bands of young people walked to and fro, singing patriotic and popular songs. There was a large crowd around the Clock Tower in Crouch End, where a fiddler kept things merry with his lively music while several tin whistle bands paraded the Hornsey High Street district'. The editorial concluded with the information that there were no dangerous fires and no arrests for drunken or disorderly behaviour. A quiet day indeed for the police court.

The reaction to the Armistice by the internees is not known. For those remaining it would be many months before the Palace gates closed behind the last prisoner. During this time repatriation continued. Its workshops shut and the building emptied, the Palace became a central clearing house as other camps closed down. The internees' tenure of the Palace would not be over until those who had not been repatriated would be moved to the tented camp at Frimley. These men would not be released from Frimley until July after the signing of the Treaty of Versailles.

In the meantime the press kept an eagle eye on doings at the Palace. Part of a snippet from *The Hornsey Journal* of 7 February 1919 reads: 'Will the spring see the people in possession of their own once more? Nothing but extreme curiosity will take them to the Palace just now. The big railway station is neither clean nor warm, and there is no temptation to walk through the Park while the snow is thick upon the ground'.

The *Wood Green Herald* of 21 March stated that 800 German prisoners had left the Palace the previous week while the *Hornsey Journal* of the same date alleged that the Palace and the Park would be re-opened to the public by Easter: 'Most of the interned aliens have been removed and at the moment we are told the Palace is practically empty. No official information is available, but we doubt very much whether there is any foundation for the rumour. In any event there will have to be extensive alterations and renovations before the public can regain occupation, and at the present rate of reconstruction this is hardly likely to be done in a few weeks'.

The *Wood Green Herald* of 4 April announced that racing was to be resumed at the Palace but denying rumours of early access to the public and confirming that a Government department was in possession. The article concludes: 'Many improvements have been made in the extensive grounds and the Grove during the closure and the Trustees are laying big plans for the future. In the meantime, racing is to be resumed this year. On the racecourse the grandstand has been improved and strengthened. This part of the grounds does not come within the regime of the military'.

The *Sentinel* of 25 April added to the speculation around the Palace's future, hinting at its public availability by August bank holiday Monday. The piece concluded with the following item: 'What's this rumour we get of Alderman Sloper giving up his part of the "Trust" which he has so splendidly carried out for so long? We hope there's nothing in it'.

The *Hornsey Journal* of 6 June confirmed this rumour, quoting Alderman Sloper as saying that he was intending to: 'devote himself to the delights of home life, which he has denied himself in the public interest for years. It was his piano playing and foreign stamps to which he hoped to turn his attention'. Sadly, these familiar pleasures were brutally curtailed by Alderman Sloper's premature death in March 1921.

The *Wood Green Herald* of 2 May, in a news item headed 'Fritz Behind Barbed Wire' reported that the previous Saturday had seen the first racing at the Palace since the outbreak of war. The article commented on the enormous number attending and the improvements (made by the internees) to the race track, grandstand and grounds. It then continues: 'The German civilians still interned at Alexandra Palace were allowed to congregate on the terrace where, behind barbed wire, they obtained a good view of the racing in the Park below.

Christmas greeting, 1918.

Notwithstanding this privilege, they had a grievance. Saturday is a visiting day and they were informed they could not invite their relatives and friends to come and join them on this occasion. Fritz considered this a great hardship'.

When news was released that the Palace would not be returned to the 'People', public fury erupted.

All to no avail. The *Hornsey Journal* of 6 June reported that in the House of Commons Sir Alfred Mond, the First Commissioner of Works, was asked by MP Godfrey Locker-Lampson on 29 May, whether Alexandra Palace would be handed back to the public. Sir Alfred replied that the Palace was being cleared in order that over 4,000 staff presently working in hotels, museums, public institutions and premises leased from businesses, would be relocated to the Palace, thus saving the Government money. He assured his questioner that the grounds would once more be available to the public. The Ministry of Munitions moved into the Palace in October 1919 and were still in possession in April 1921. It was not until October 1919 that the grounds were surrendered to the Trustees. The barbed wire was not cleared away until long after that date.

The Sentinel of 1 August reported that Alderman Sloper conducted a party of London and local pressmen around the Palace and Park to convince them that the grounds – still enveloped in long coils of rusting barbed wire and uneven from the internees' allotments – could not be opened to the public at present. The newspaper described some of the allotments still containing vegetables and flowers grown by the prisoners. The grounds had been much improved by the internees, the old fairground being demolished, with new lawns and a rose garden made. A bowling green was in the process of being created while in the Grove a new path was lined with trees, a new bandstand and refreshment pavilion erected. For their labours the internees had been paid 3 ha'pennys an hour, which covered the cost of cigarettes and other small luxuries.

The Palace itself was in a very dilapidated state. No maintenance work had been done on the building since it had been taken over by the Government in 1914. Many panes of glass from the Palace roof were broken or missing, rain leaking everywhere and allowing access to pigeons. Woodwork was smashed and bereft of paint while floors were badly affected with dry rot. The Great Hall was dingy from the fumes of many oil stoves and cigarette smoke while the statues of the Kings and Queens of England were in a filthy, damaged state. The remainder of the building was in no better condition. The Palace was described as a 'scene of the utmost desolation'.

The Great Organ was choked with fluff and dust from the hundreds of blankets and carbon from the oil stoves and, upon examination, had been badly damaged. Rooms below the organ had been broken into and ransacked, parts of the mechanism and organ pipes had been torn from their fittings and used to bludgeon other pipes, with some thrown into the Great Hall itself. Others were found along the railway track leading from Alexandra Palace to King's Cross. The perpetrators were soldiers from the Palace who, when apprehended, were court martialled.

Wandering around with the reporters Alderman Sloper mused that some of the internees were really 'very decent'. One, whose lordly pleasures in freedom were taken 'up the Thames' was content in old clothing to punt on the lake and clear it of weeds. Another was happy tree cutting. There were those with English wives and sons fighting in the

The rose garden created by internees on the site of the old fairground.

The Grove, restored by internees, c. 1920.

British Army, whom even Alderman Sloper would not deport offhand without some sifting. They were objects of pity he said, when you really knew them. Alderman Sloper concluded: 'What a pity we are not all more determined to be kindly men rather than what, geographically, we happen to be born'.

The grounds were re-opened in 1920, and part of the Palace opened to the public in 1922. A tram celebrated the re-opening by running away down the hill and hitting a stationary tram at Wood Green Gate. There were no serious injuries. The Great Hall remained closed because of its leaking roof and lack of modern heating.

At the Golden Jubilee celebrations in May 1923, commemorative tablets were unveiled on the south front to Alderman Burt and the late Alderman Sloper. The programme says: 'The magnitude of Mr Sloper's task is only just being realised, and it is the regret of all that he was not spared to see the Palace he loved so well take its stand, as it does today, in the very front rank of England's showplaces'.

Also within the Golden Jubilee's programme pages were lists of the day's and future's events. While promising the return of organ recitals and other delights, the programme refers to the partially restored Palace as already offering 'warmth, light and comfort taking the place of disorder and ruin'.

Opposite, above: *The refurbished theatre – view from stage, 1923.*

Opposite, below: *Scout jamboree in the grounds, 1922. This was attended by the Prince of Wales, later Edward VIII.*

An aerial view of Alexandra Palace in 1928, showing the railway station, racecourse and, in the bottom left-hand corner of the picture, part of the bowling green made by the internees.

❧ EPILOGUE ❧

Sadly, by the early 1930s 'disorder and ruin' once more prevailed, with the situation desperate. The roller-skating rink and ballroom in the Banqueting Hall remained popular but many theatrical productions flopped badly, with reports of artistes sometimes playing to an empty house.

The Palace was saved by the public television service inaugurated in 1935 by the BBC. Chosen in preference to Hampstead Heath and Crystal Palace, the television studio in the south-east tower began broadcasting in November 1936, successfully transmitting the Coronation of King George VI in 1937. The Palace played little part in the Second World War. In 1944 a flying bomb exploded to the north of the building, damaging the roof of the Great Hall. The organ suffered water penetration and, covered in snow, had to be dismantled during the severe winter of 1946/47.

Eventually the Great Hall was restored, the BBC resumed televised broadcasts and the roller-skating rink re-opened only to close for good in 1974 because of the dangerous state of the roof. The race track was closed and the grandstand demolished while the Banqueting Hall, which had been used by a clothing firm during the war, burnt down. The final straw came on 10 July 1980 when the Palace ignited for the second time. About half of the building was completely destroyed. After many travails the Palace re-opened to the public on 17 March 1988.

And so today, the Monster of Muswell Hill sits upon its hilltop perch, battered by over 130 years of crises which are still, even now, dogging the fortunes of the People's Palace. The curse lives on.

INDEX

AIR RAIDS 55, 66, 68, 74

AIRSHIP 30, 32, 34-5, 68

ALEXANDRA PALACE

ALEXANDRA PARK 10, 11, 15, 22, 25

ALIEN ENEMIES 42, 51-2, 58, 107

ALIENS RESTRICTION ACT 1914 42, 46, 63

ALLOTMENTS 97, 120

ANTI-GERMAN 44, 74

ARMY 41-2, 45, 54, 60, 72, 86, 104, 106, 111, 118

ASQUITH, HERBERT (PRIME MINISTER) 63

ATROCITIES (GERMAN) 52-4, 56

AUSTRIA 46, 51, 56, 70-1

AUSTRO-HUNGARIAN EMPIRE 46

BALDWIN, PROFESSOR 23-4, 38

BALLOON ASCENTS 39, 47

BANK HOLIDAYS 19, 36, 38

BANQUETING HALL 18, 29, 31, 125

BARBED-WIRE DISEASE 86

BARTON, DR 31-2, 34-5

BATTALIONS 62, 79, 83-5, 97-8

BBC 125

BELGIANS 51, 53-8, 60, 62, 64, 67

BELGIUM 47, 56, 69

BIG BEN 42, 117

BOTTOMLEY, HORATIO 64, 68

BRITISH MEDICAL JOURNAL 78

BOSTON, LINCOLNSHIRE 114

Bull, John 46, 56-7, 60, 64, 69, 72, 74

BURT, HENRY 25-6, 36

'CAMP VOGEL' 86

CHRISTMAS 37, 45, 47, 51, 57-8, 67, 70, 80-8, 95, 119

CENTRAL COUNCIL OF THE UNITED ALIENS
  RELIEF SOCIETIES 60

CINEMA 101

COAL (SEE ALSO FUEL) 51, 58, 60, 82, 114

COHEN-PORTHEIM, PAUL 71, 77-8, 90

COLONIAL TROOPS 27-9

CONCERTS 18, 20, 22, 31, 49, 57, 69, 92, 97, 101

CONAN DOYLE, ARTHUR 107

CORONATION, KING EDWARD VII'S 27, 29

Daily Mail 72, 83, 90

Daily Sketch 69

DEATHS 15, 58, 90, 93

DEFENCE OF THE REALM ACT (DORA) 45, 67

DIVORCE 88, 103, 107

DIVORCE LAW REFORM UNION 107

DOUGLAS, ISLE OF MAN 71

ERFURT, FRANZ 94

FAIRGROUND 121

FIRE (FIRST PALACE) 12-16

FIREWORK DISPLAYS 19, 24-5, 33, 38, 47

FOOD 19-20, 40, 43, 45, 53, 58, 71-7, 78-9, 86, 89-91,
  101, 105-6

FOX HUNTING 23

FRITH HILL (FRIMLEY) 54

FROWDE-WALKER, LT COL 92, 94, 96

FUEL (SEE ALSO COAL) 5 8, 105-6

FUNERALS 77, 93, 106

GERMANS 46, 48, 52, 54-7, 62-4, 67-72, 82, 84, 90,
  107

GERMANY 40, 42, 46-7, 56-7, 68-9, 79, 82, 101, 104,
  108, 116

GREAT HALL 7, 20-1, 24-5, 28, 31-2, 35, 37, 49, 53,
  57-8, 83, 85, 120, 122, 125

GROVE (THE ESTATE) 10

GROVE (ALEXANDRA PALACE) 11, 18, 27, 32, 47, 49-50,
  119-21

HORNSEY 9, 32-3, 67, 118

Hornsey Journal 32, 36-7, 49, 60, 68-9, 118-20

HORSES 18, 27, 42, 48

HORSE RACING 10, 24

HOUSE OF COMMONS 63, 68, 90, 93, 120

HUGHES, W.R. - (THE SOCIETY OF FRIENDS
  EMERGENCY RELIEF COMMITTEE) 70, 79-80, 86, 93

HUNGARIANS 46

INTERNMENT 7, 57, 63-4, 70, 72-3, 75, 77, 84, 90, 92-3,
  96, 98, 105, 108, 114

ISLE OF MAN 63, 70-2, 78, 82, 84, 88, 92-3, 95, 107-8

M KÄSTNER, CHAIR, DR MÄRKEL'S COMMITTEE 97

KAISER 68, 74, 117

KING EDWARD'S HORSE 49

KING GEORGE V 37, 125

KITCHENER, LORD 45, 90
KNOCKALOE (ISLE OF MAN) 71, 79, 88, 107
KRUGER, PRESIDENT 35

LIGHTING RESTRICTIONS 54
LOCAL GOVERNMENT BOARD (LGB) 51, 109, 111
LONDON COUNTY ASYLUM, COLNEY HATCH 86
LONG TOM GUN 34-5

McDONAGH, MICHAEL 41, 45, 63, 82-3, 86
MALNUTRITION 101, 107
Manchester Guardian 46, 109
METROPOLITAN ASYLUM BOARD (MAB) 51, 60
MILITARY GUARDS 64, 67, 75, 114
MUSWELL HILL 9-11, 15, 17, 19, 23, 31-3, 53, 57, 69, 125

North Middlesex Chronicle 23, 30, 32, 35-6, 38, 67
NOTSCHKE, RICHARD 72, 75, 77, 78, 84, 89, 113, 116

ORGAN, HENRY WILLIS 12-3, 17-8, 21, 25, 36-7, 46, 49-50, 69, 84, 120, 122, 125

PANKHURST, SYLVIA 72, 75, 104-5
PARLIAMENT 19, 41-2, 45, 48, 117
PIGEONS (CARRIER) 18, 52, 120
POLICE 17, 42, 46, 48, 51-2, 54, 57, 60, 64, 68-70, 75, 77, 104-5, 117-8
POOR LAW 58, 107-8, 110
POOR LAW GUARDIANS 104-5
POTATO HARVEST 89
PRINCE OF WALES (VISIT TO PALACE IN 1876) 19-20 (VISIT TO SCOUT JAMBOREE IN 1922) 122
PRISON SHIPS 71, 73
PRISONERS OF WAR 7, 75, 84

QUAKER EMERGENCY COMMITTEE FOR THE ASSISTANCE OF GERMANS, AUSTRIANS AND HUNGARIANS IN DISTRESS 46
QUEEN ALEXANDRA (THE QUEEN MOTHER) 54
QUEEN MARY 37, 53

RAILWAYS 32, 45
RED CROSS 114, 116
RELIGIOUS SOCIETY OF FRIENDS 46
REPATRIATION 79, 95, 101, 115, 117
ROCKER, RUDOLF 79-80, 84, 86, 88, 90, 92-3, 95-6, 99, 101, 103

ROLLER-SKATING RINK 27, 47, 49, 125
RUSSIAN SOLDIERS 54

ST STEPHEN'S HOUSE 106
SAUTER, PROFESSOR GEORG 101
SAUTER, RUDOLF 101
SLOPER, ALDERMAN EDWIN 37-8, 40, 49, 57-8, 62, 67-8, 119-20, 122
SOCIETY FOR THE RELIEF OF DISTRESSED FOREIGNERS 109, 111
SOCIETY OF FRIENDS OF FOREIGNERS IN DISTRESS 60
SPALDING, LINCOLNSHIRE 113
SPIES 42, 45, 48, 52, 57, 63, 68
SPY MANIA 48
STRATFORD CAMP (EAST LONDON) 75, 77-8, 84
SWISS EMBASSY/SWISS LEGATION 86, 93
SWITCHBACK 47, 68

TELEVISION 7-8, 125
THEATRE 7, 16, 18, 22, 26, 32, 40, 49, 53, 61, 97, 101, 123
Times, The 10-11, 41-2, 45-6, 53, 60, 79, 82, 107
TOTTENHAM 9-10, 15, 17, 31, 46, 52, 54, 56, 68, 90
Tottenham and Edmonton Herald 68
TRAMS 32, 35, 38, 117-8
TRUSTEES – ALEXANDRA PALACE 7, 25-8, 31-2, 35-7, 40, 48-51, 62, 67-70, 119-20
TURK, CARL (CHARLIE) 7, 108, 118
TURK, CHARLES (CHAZ) 109
TURK, ELLEN 108, 110
TURK, OLIVE 108-9

VERSAILLES, TREATY OF 109, 118
VISCHER, DR A.L. 86

WANDA, GUSTAVE 97
WAR OFFICE 27, 46-7, 50, 52, 67, 69
WATER SUPPLY 17
Women's Dreadnought, The 104
Wood Green Herald 52-4, 56, 60, 64, 67-70, 82, 92-3, 118-9
Wood Green Sentinel 27, 48
WORKHOUSE 46, 63, 86, 105, 107, 109, 113

YMCA HUT 95-6

ZEPPELINS 50, 58

Other local titles published by Tempus

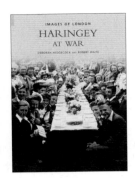

Haringey at War

DEBORAH HEDGECOCK AND ROBERT WAITE

This collection of photographs from Bruce Castle Museum offers a pictorial record of the wartime history of the London Borough of Haringey, highlighting important events for the former boroughs of Tottenham, Hornsey and Wood Green, as well as life-changing events for its residents. Aspects of everyday life are also featured, from the destruction of homes and the trials of rationing, to land girls, Belgian refugees and air-raid shelters.

0-7524-3297-4

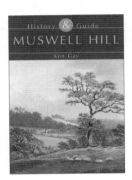

Haringey Pubs

CHRIS AND HAZEL WHITEHOUSE

This informative volume recalls the many varied roles pubs have played in the social life of Haringey during the last two centuries. Illustrated with over 170 old images, drawn from the archive of Bruce Castle Museum, each picture offers an insight into the popularity and changing role of Haringey's pubs. Those featured include The Gate House in Highgate, The Spurs pub and Tottenham's fourteenth-century Bull Inn.

0 7524 3296 6

Muswell Hill

KEN GAY

Not urbanized until the end of the nineteenth century, Muswell Hill was quickly built up as a middle class Edwardian suburb with shopping parades, domestic houses set in tree-lined avenues and many churches. In this volume Ken Gay uses over150 views to illuminate Muswell Hill's unfolding story. In addition a guided tour introduces routes by which the suburb's past and present can be explored.

0 7524 2604 4

London: Life in the Post-War Years

DOUGLAS WHITWORTH

These evocative images of London were taken in the years immediately following the Second World War, and are the work of Douglas Whitworth who took many photographs of people, places and events in the capital during this period. The pictures capture the atmosphere of the time, and also feature a succession of nostalgic views around some of London's most famous streets and landmarks, including Petticoat Lane and Speaker's Corner.

0 7524 2816 0

If you are interested in purchasing other books published by Tempus, or in case you have difficulty finding any Tempus books in your local bookshop, you can also place orders directly through our website

www.tempus-publishing.com